Clean Heart, Renewed Joy

A Six Week Journey through Psalm 51

Sue Badeau

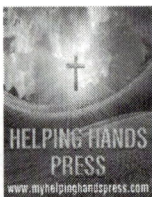

Helping Hands Press
922 S. Woodbourne Road, Suite 153
Levittown, PA 19056

First Edition

For discounts on bulk purchases, please email
contactus@myhelpinghandspress.com

Printed in the United States of America

ISBN:978-1-62208-580-4

Table of Contents

Introduction

Does Psalm 51 stir your soul as it does mine? Like me, do you long for that "clean heart" and "renewed joy" promised in these familiar verses? This Psalm contains a perfect and complete framework, divided into six themes, for the Christian walk of continual renewal, growth and purpose. The themes, reflected throughout the Psalm include:

(1) God's Holiness
(2) Our Separation From God
(3) Thorough Cleansing
(4) Truth in the Inner Being
(5) Joy
(6) Purpose

Grasping the first five themes requires study, deep reflection and soul-searching. The final theme, purpose, is highlighted by that marvelous phrase, "And then . ." –demonstrating that the inner renewal and joy is not only for personal growth and spiritual development, but also for a purpose, for the "and then" that comes afterward.

This book, organized around the six themes listed above, is a perfect devotional for Lent or any other time you want to embark on a season of reflection and renewal. Each week begins with a day to meditate on Psalm 51 in its entirety and then includes several days of closer meditation on one or two verses. This approach provides opportunities to grasp overall themes and context while also digging deeper into key ideas and pearls of wisdom. I invite you to walk with me for six weeks, reflecting upon and allowing God to work within you in each of these six areas. Begin expectantly and come away refreshed and re-invigorated with a renewed sense of joy and purpose!

Getting the Most Out of This Book

Have you ever taken a road trip? I have. One thing I know is that the trip will be more successful, meaningful and memorable if I prepare well ahead of time and carry a good tool kit. In order to make the most of this journey through Psalm 51, I encourage you to prepare well and bring the right tools. Here are a few tips to help ensure that your journey will be successful, meaningful and memorable.

Preparation:

Follow this simple "A, B, C" plan to prepare yourself for the journey ahead:

Approach your journey with prayer. Invite God to be your navigator and tour guide as your travel this road. Begin the entire series with a prayer that God will open your mind, eyes, heart and spirit to new insights, wisdom and "aha" moments that will spur growth, action and meaningful change in your life. Begin each day with that same prayer, and end each day and the series with a prayer that God will show you the connections you can make between the lessons you have learned here and real-life opportunities for application.

Bring your whole self to this journey. Be fully present, fully awake, fully aware and fully honest each day when you sit down to read your daily reflection. Select a time of day and a place where you can engage with the material in this book in that spirit of wholeheartedness and honesty.

Commit yourself to completing the entire journey. This book is designed to be completed in six weeks of daily readings. However, life happens. If you are cruising along reading daily and then something interrupts you, don't worry. Just come back to it when you can. You may not finish in exactly six weeks. But do finish. While each reflection is written in such a way that it can stand alone, the full value of this series of devotionals will only be realized when you complete the entire journey, whether in six weeks or eight or ten. Commit yourself to crossing the finish line.

Tools:

In addition to this book itself, there are four other basic tools that will help you glean the most from your walk on this path:

Multiple Versions of the Bible: Unless otherwise noted, the Bible passages quoted here are taken from the New American Standard Bible (NASB). However, you will see throughout the book that I have occasionally drawn from other versions as a way to gain fresh perspective or new insight on a particular passage. Bring your favorite Bible with you each day as you sit down to read the daily reflection, but also have a tool such as **www.biblegateway.com** or **www.biblehub.com** at your fingertips to enhance your ability to dig deeper into the text.

A Journal: Each day's reading ends with a question for reflection. Use a journal (an old-fashioned notebook and pen or a folder on your computer or tablet, or even the "notes" pages on your smart phone) to record your reflections. Go back and re-read them from time to time, even after you have completed this journey. Add new insights, thoughts or questions along the way. Using a journal helps you to become a continual learner, an explorer always ready for the next discovery.

Music: Each reading suggests a piece of music for you to listen to at the end of your daily study. Music deepens and broadens your understanding of the passage as well as your ability to make connections between the words on the page and opportunities for action in real life. Associating music with learning also helps to root the lessons learned more deeply in your memory and assist with recall in the future. Be prepared and equipped to listen to the suggested music or music of your choosing each day.

Images: In addition to associating your daily reflections with music, including visual images that have personal meaning in your own life will bring value to your study. The images may include photos or other forms of artwork and visual expression.

The cover selected for this book demonstrates the value of images. In the spring of 2012 my husband and I experienced the death of one of our sons. We were in a deep season of grief when dear friends provided us with an opportunity to spend a long weekend at their cottage on a lake. We embraced this opportunity for a personal retreat and prayed that God would use it to guide us out of the valley of grief and into the next phase of our life journey. The first morning we were there, I went outside for a walk along the lake. It had rained the night before. I noticed raindrops clinging to tiny buds of yet-to-be-born flowers. This image stirred a great sense of hope and joy within my spirit. This simple image captured the promise and power of cleansing, renewal and new life. Every time I see this image I am reminded of the gift of hope and insight God gave to me on that day. When I embarked again on a study of Psalm 51, this image came to mind and symbolized the essence of the lessons I took away. While I hope that you will enjoy this particular image, I pray that God will provide each of you with your own image or images that can serve as powerful reminders of God's love, mercy and grace in your own life.

Day 1 – Beginning

Read Psalm 51

Be gracious to me, O God, according to Your lovingkindness; According to the greatness of Your compassion blot out my transgressions. ² Wash me thoroughly from my iniquity and cleanse me from my sin. ³ For I know my transgressions, And my sin is ever before me. ⁴ Against You, You only, I have sinned And done what is evil in Your sight, So that You are justified when You speak And blameless when You judge.

⁵ Behold, I was brought forth in iniquity, And in sin my mother conceived me. ⁶ Behold, You desire truth in the innermost being, And in the hidden part You will make me know wisdom. ⁷ Purify me with hyssop, and I shall be clean; Wash me, and I shall be whiter than snow. ⁸ Make me to hear joy and gladness, Let the bones which You have broken rejoice. ⁹ Hide Your face from my sins And blot out all my iniquities.

¹⁰ Create in me a clean heart, O God, and renew a steadfast spirit within me. ¹¹ Do not cast me away from Your presence And do not take Your Holy Spirit from me. ¹² Restore to me the joy of Your salvation And sustain me with a willing spirit. ¹³ Then I will teach transgressors Your ways, And sinners will be converted to You.

¹⁴ Deliver me from bloodguiltiness, O God, the God of my salvation; Then my tongue will joyfully sing of Your righteousness. ¹⁵ O Lord, open my lips, That my mouth may declare Your praise. ¹⁶ For You do not delight in sacrifice, otherwise I would give it; You are not pleased with burnt offering. ¹⁷ *The sacrifices of God are a broken spirit; A broken and a contrite heart, O God, You will not despise.*

¹⁸ *By Your favor do good to Zion;* [n]*Build the walls of Jerusalem.* ¹⁹ *Then You will delight in* ʲ *righteous sacrifices, In burnt offering and whole burnt offering; Then young bulls will be offered on Your altar.*

Begin today by reading Psalm 51 in its entirety. Use a parallel Bible reading tool and read it three or four times in different translations. Ask God to give you eyes to see and ears to hear it anew as if you are reading it for the first time. As you reflect, listen to the stirring rendition in music, by Keith Green.
(https://www.youtube.com/watch?v=rv16YUTCp9U& feature=kp)

Ask God to prepare your heart to receive His life-giving words over the next six weeks. Take a few minutes to write in your journal—what are your "first-impressions-all-over-again" of this Psalm? What is one hope you have for how God will speak to you and renew your spirit during this season of reflection?

Day 2 – Introduction to Theme 1

"God's Holiness"
Read Verses 1, 11 and 18-19

Be gracious to me, O God, according to Your lovingkindness; According to the greatness of Your compassion blot out my transgressions. V.1

Do not cast me away from Your presence And do not take Your Holy Spirit from me. V.11

By Your favor do good to Zion; Build the walls of Jerusalem. Then You will delight in righteous sacrifices, In burnt offering and whole burnt offering; Then young bulls will be offered on Your altar. V. 18-19

In most Bibles, these words precede the beginning of the Psalm:

A Contrite Sinner's Prayer for Pardon.

For the choir director. A Psalm of David, when Nathan the prophet came to him, after he had gone in to Bathsheba.

This Psalm is loaded with language about sin. It was written after David was confronted with the depth, darkness and magnitude of some of the most despicable sins he had committed in his lifetime. He was miserable.

We've all been there. Maybe even this morning. So deep in the pit of our sin that we can't see any light at all. Enveloped in darkness.

And it is in this very moment of nearly hopeless despair that the Psalm begins not with language about the greatness of our sin (that will come later) but with language about the greatness of our God. In studying this Psalm, the first thing I must comprehend is that it is because of God's mercy, his unfailing love, his great compassion and his favor that I can be forgiven from my sins and go on to experience the inner truth, joy and purpose that this Psalm speaks of.

It is not because of anything about me. It is not because I am basically a good person and worthy of his redemption. It is not because of all the great things I have done in my life or that I am better than anyone else. It is truly all about, only about God's great mercy, love and compassion.

As I reflect upon the verses for this week, I begin to think about the story of the Titanic. The captain of the ship was doing everything he could to save the ship—why? For the wood and metal and cargo? No, of course not—but for the people, the lives of the people. He had mercy and love and compassion for the people, and he did not want any to be lost.

And yet because it is a human story, it is filled with failure. The captain failed, and the people failed to act with mercy and kindness and compassion. They allowed those deemed to be more worthy to get to the lifeboats first, and those considered less worthy were consigned to steerage and likely not even to get a life vest never mind a seat in the life boat.

Sometimes, I believe our human brains construct an image of God like the flawed captain and others on the Titanic—choosing whether we get "in the lifeboat" of his mercy, love and forgiveness because of some quality we have in ourselves. If we paid to be in the first class cabin we can be saved, but if we are in steerage, too bad.

And yet, of course, God is not like that at all. All have the opportunity to be saved, whether we are in the "first class" or "steerage" sections of life, it is because of God's unfailing love and great compassion that we can be forgiven and saved. He does not just have love and compassion; he has those qualities beyond measure— his love does not fail. His compassion is greater than our imagination, greater than our sins; he will not cast us into the depths of the sea without a life vest. He will not cast us away from his presence at all. His Holy Spirit will never leave us and his favor will rest upon us.

We will examine these verses in more depth this week, but for today, reflect on them as a trio and write a few notes in your journal describing what God's unfailing compassion and holiness mean to you.

As you do, listen to your favorite version of "Amazing Grace." Here is one I like:

https://www.youtube.com/watch?v=Cgwn1vjNHjE

Day 3 – Lovingkindness

Read Verse 1(a)

Be gracious to me, O God, according to Your lovingkindness;

Today, let's focus on the word translated here as "lovingkindness." In other translations this is also translated as constant love, steadfast love and unfailing love.

Love that does not, cannot and will not fail.

We live in a world where nothing is constant and everything fails.

We've all heard the statistic that nearly half of all marriages end in divorce—do we realize this means 6646 divorces per day in our country?

On any given day there are 400,000 children in our nation's foster care system, and each year over 23,000 of these children "age out" of the system with no family—no one to care for them at all.

These are just two examples demonstrating that in our homes, in our families, in our communities love is rarely constant; love frequently fails. If we add in statistics about child trafficking, domestic violence and homelessness the weight of love's failure is staggering.

As I seek to love and minister to others in the face of such brokenness, how can I possibly truly comprehend the depth and reality of God's unfailing love?

I pray that during this period of reflection and prayer, I will come to know, experience and be utterly astonished by the depths of God's unfailing, constant and steadfast love, and I pray that you will be astonished too!

Take a moment to reflect on what "unfailing" love means in your life and jot some notes in your journal.

A song for reflection today is "Unfailing Love" **https://www.youtube.com/watch?v=SheFMy98pqk**

Day 4 – Great Compassion

Read Verse 1(b),

According to the greatness of Your compassion blot out my transgressions.

God's compassion is great enough for me, even when I feel totally unworthy. I am unworthy, but that is exactly the point—God's love and compassion are great enough, even for me, even in my unworthiness.

The story found in Nehemiah chapter nine is particularly stunning regarding this point. I encourage you to read the entire chapter. Count the number of times you read the word "compassion" in this chapter. Over and over again, the people had been so disobedient and rebellious that God decides to hand them over to their enemies. And yet, over and over again he is moved "in his great compassion" to rescue his people from their enemies.

Each time, the people go immediately back to the ways of sin—verse twenty-eight *"But as soon as they had rest, they did evil again before You;"*

Like children! Any parent, teacher, auntie or coach knows the frustration of spending time teaching, reprimanding and lovingly disciplining a child only to see her return to the same behaviors moments later.

As a mom, these are the moments that make me pull my hair out. "How many times have I told you ..." is a tired, trite but very real phrase on the lips of any adult who provides care and guidance for children.

As a foster and adoptive parent, I know that children will do more of this testing when they are uncertain if they can trust you. Again and again they will engage in actions and behaviors that they know are against your family rules and values. And again and again, out of love and compassion, you will discipline, teach and then wrap up the interaction by saying, "I still love you; I will always love you."

As the child becomes more secure in the relationship, the frequency of the testing diminishes. The child begins to trust that nothing they can do is going to push you over the edge and cause you to "send them back." They can rest in the assurance of your love and that is when their healing begins and hope blossoms.

How often am I like that insecure foster child? Testing, testing, testing God. Daring Him to turn away and "send me back" into the dark abyss. Yet, in God's great compassion He forgives me, rescues me, and preserves my life.

Will you pray with me? *"Lord help me today and always to remember that I can trust you and rest in the assurance of your great compassion for me. Help me to test you less and trust you more. Help me also to have and to show this great compassion towards each precious child you place in my life. 'Remember not the sins of my youth, and my rebellious ways; according to your love, remember me, for you are good, O Lord.' (Psalm 25:7) Amen."*

Take a few moments to reflect upon God's great compassion and make some notes in your journal.

As you reflect, listen to this rendition of "God of Mercy and Compassion"
https://www.youtube.com/watch?v=OQV60w3DX00

11

Day 5 – Presence

Read Verse 11

Do not cast me away from Your presence And do not take Your Holy Spirit from me.

Read also:

Exodus 33:15 Then Moses said to him, "If your Presence does not go with us, do not send us up from here.

And

Psalm 138:8 The LORD will fulfill his purpose for me; your love, O LORD, endures forever— do not abandon the works of your hands.

For many children, the worst possible consequence they can receive is to be "cast away" from the presence of their parent, siblings, schoolmates or others that they love and look up to. This is why "go to your room," and "time out" have been standard parenting tools for generations, and missing recess or being sent to the principal's office is the school-based version.

Studying Psalm 51, I've already been reminded that my sins can be forgiven and indeed "blotted out" not due to any worthiness on my part, but rather due to the unfailing love and great compassion of our God. As I meditate on and respond to the depth of that love and the generosity of that compassion, it is no wonder that I want to bask in His presence forever.

"Do not cast me away!" is the cry of my heart as I cling to my one true anchor.

Reading further in the Exodus passage, I feel as Moses does, *"Lord if whatever it is I am about to do is not only ordained by you but fully accompanied by your presence— then please, just don't send me!"*

Whether I walk out the door to speak to an audience of thousands at a big conference, or to one teacher at my child's school, I know that without the Holy Spirit at my side, stepping before me, having my back and filling my heart, mind, ears and lips, my efforts will be futile and fear will fill the vacuum.

"Do not take your Holy Spirit from me!" is the cry of my heart as I step out in faith to be about my Father's business.

I am both comforted and emboldened with confidence knowing that indeed, He who has preserved my life because of his unfailing love and great compassion will neither abandon me, nor send me out without the full armor of His presence and His Spirit.

Psalm 138 reminds me again that I can have this confidence not because of my talents and skills, but because He has a purpose for me and I am one of the many works of His hand, so how could He abandon His own creation?

His love endures forever.

I now take a different approach to discipline with children, particularly those who have experienced trauma, grief or loss. Instead of "time out" I consign them to "time-in" when they are in trouble. Time they must spend at my side, doing whatever I am doing, perhaps missing out on a TV show or game they would rather be playing. But during this "time in" they learn that I will never cast them away nor abandon them, even when they are misbehaved and at their worst.

This is the discipline our Lord seeks as well. When we are struggling, misbehaving, allowing sin to overtake us, he calls us to "time in." Time to sit at his side, absorb the fullness of His presence and re-learn the lesson that He will never cast us away— His love endures forever.

Have there been times in your life when you have feared being "cast away" from God's presence? Reflect on this and consider how you can spend more "time-in" with Him when these fearful moments occur. Jot a few notes in your journal as you absorb the power of this truth: *He will never cast you away. His love endures forever.* Amen.

A beautiful hymn that always reminds me of God's abiding presence is "In the Garden"
https://www.youtube.com/watch?v=_2eSfKqMRbA

13

Day 6 – Spirit

Read Verse 11

Do not cast me away from Your presence and do not take Your Holy Spirit from me.

We are going to linger on verse eleven for one more day. Yesterday, we focused on God's presence, today on the second half of the verse: *"take not your Holy Spirit from me."*

I gain new insight into this portion of the verse when I read it as interpreted in The Message and the New Living Bible:

"Do not fail to breathe holiness in me". V 11(b) in The Message

"Don't take your Spirit of Holiness from me." v 11 (b) New Living Bible

The Holy Spirit is many things to the believer—comforter, enabler, guide, internal accountability partner, gift-giver and more. But in this passage a particular role of the Holy Spirit is highlighted—the one who "breathes Holiness" into me.

Leviticus 11:44 (reiterated in I Peter 1:16) roughly translated as *"be holy as I am holy"* has always been a sticking point for me in my Christian walk. How can I, a sinner, be holy?

The answer is simple—on my own, I cannot. I can confess my sins a hundred, or even a thousand times a day and still not be holy. I can deny myself and lift my cross attempting to carry it a hundred times, yea a thousand times a day and still I will not be holy.

Holiness is so far above my pay grade I cannot even aspire to it in this lifetime.

And yet . . . God calls me to be holy. **To *be* holy.** Not merely to imitate his holiness. Not to strive after it or set it afore me as a goal. No—God simply says, *"Be Holy."*

I know that it is not an effective parenting strategy to tell children to "be good" and then expect "goodness" to follow; yet it is such an easy phrase to fall back on. *"We are going to the grocery store, be good." "We are going to visit Grandma, she is not feeling well, so please, be good." "I'm making an important phone call, just stay in the playroom and be good."* Sound familiar?

An impossible standard, one that is guaranteed to disappoint. Is this our God—creating impossible standards and setting both Himself and us up for disappointment time and time again?

On the days when I feel this way, the best antidote is to return here, to Psalm 51, verse eleven and quietly pray, *"Oh Lord, I cannot be Holy on my own, but you desire holiness. Thank you that you breathe your spirit of Holiness into me each and every time I turn my heart and face toward you. Do not, dear Lord, do not ever take your Holy Spirit from me—breathe your spirit of Holiness into me this day and every day. Amen."*

As we close our time together today, listen to the hymn, "Breathe on Me Breath of God" **http://www.youtube.com/watch?v=4VMzzvz1aAw** - Reflect on this quote about Holiness from Mother Theresa as you jot in your journal a few notes about what "being Holy" means to you:

"Holiness does not consist in doing extraordinary things. It consists in accepting, with a smile, what Jesus sends us. It consists in accepting and following the will of God.[1]"

---

[1] *Goodreads*. Web. 6 Feb. 2015. <http://www.goodreads.com/quotes/203154-holiness-does-not-consist-in-doing-extraordinary-things-it-consists>.

Day 7 – Offering

Read Verses 18-19

By Your favor do good to Zion; Build the walls of Jerusalem. Then You will delight in righteous sacrifices, In burnt offering and whole burnt offering; Then young bulls will be offered on Your altar.

As many times as I've read Psalm 51, I've wished it ended with verse seventeen. Verse seventeen (which we'll come to later in our study) is such a perfect ending, why go on after that? Particularly with verses that highlight burnt offerings and sacrificing bulls?

For years, I've struggled to figure out where these two verses fit. Thankfully, God responded to my prayers and clearly showed me that these verses perfectly wrap up our first theme, the theme of God's overwhelming, unfailing love and holiness.

What do burnt offerings have to do with it? As I pondered this, my mind wandered back to a day nearly thirty years ago. My husband and I took most of our children from our Cabot, VT farmhouse into town for a day of activities. One of our oldest sons, a recently adopted teenager, asked to stay home. He had been sulky and in some ways resistant to participating in the life of the family. He balked at doing things "our way" and staying home from a family outing seemed to be just one more example of his rejection.

When we returned from our outing he greeted us at the door with a huge smile. He was bursting with pride and excitement to show us what he had done while we were gone.

"I cleaned out the basement!" he exclaimed, "I burnt all the trash—look how clean and neat it is now!" Horrified I looked towards our incinerator—smoke billowing skyward. There had been no trash in the basement, rather trash bags and boxes filled with old baby clothes, blankets, photo albums and other irreplaceable and sentimentally valuable items. All were gone.

Yet, instead of anger, I was overcome with love. Somehow, his actions touched me deeply and found that place of favor in my heart. With smoke still stinging my eyes, I gave him a hug. I accepted his "burnt offering" and saw something new in his eyes—a new and deeper love of family and desire to be part of our life and our way. God's favor upon our family was evident that day in new and fresh ways.

"By your favor do good " verse eighteen begins. This is reminiscent of the words in verse one: *"according to Your lovingkindness"* and *"according to the greatness of Your compassion."* Verse eighteen brings us full-circle - we began by contemplating the depth and generosity of God's unfailing love and compassion, and wrap up by understanding that it is the magnitude of His favor that brings about holiness in our lives and in our world.

References here to Zion and Jerusalem remind us of God's desire for both earthly and heavenly kingdoms—where His peace and justice will rule and reign. Where the lion will indeed lie down with the lamb, where every sword will be turned to a plowshare. Where there are no more tears and everyone that is hungry will be filled. Where there is neither Jew nor Greek, male nor female, master or slave—but all are precious and beloved and valued.

And just as the beginning of this Psalm reminds us that our own sins are forgiven not due to our own worthiness but as a result of God's great and enduring love and compassion, so the Psalm ends with a reminder that our collective sins as a world filled with flawed people who wage war and sow injustice will only be forgiven, God's holy kingdom will be restored and the new Jerusalem will be built as a result of His favor, not our good works, political beliefs or loudly raised voices.

When His favor covers the land once again, then, and only then will he accept the sacrifices and offerings we bring to His throne.

As we close out our first week in Psalm 51, reflect on God's desire to see His kingdom come on earth as it is in heaven. Pray for grace to be one of His workers in bringing about His favor for our own cities and broken world. What offering can you bring today?

Today's hymn is "Here I Am Lord" **https://www.youtube.com/watch?v=EcxOkht8w7c**

Day 8 – Behold

Read Psalm 51

We have completed the first week in our study, focused on the theme of God's Holiness. As we prepare our hearts for week two, which, beginning tomorrow, will focus on the theme, "Our Separation from God" let's take a moment today to go back and read the entire Psalm again.

Be gracious to me, O God, according to Your lovingkindness; According to the greatness of Your compassion blot out my transgressions. ²Wash me thoroughly from my iniquity And cleanse me from my sin. ³For I know my transgressions, And my sin is ever before me. ⁴Against You, You only, I have sinned And done what is evil in Your sight, So that You are justified when You speak And blameless when You judge.

⁵Behold, I was brought forth in iniquity, And in sin my mother conceived me. ⁶Behold, You desire truth in the innermost being, And in the hidden part You will make me know wisdom. ⁷Purify me with hyssop, and I shall be clean; Wash me, and I shall be whiter than snow. ⁸Make me to hear joy and gladness, Let the bones which You have broken rejoice. ⁹Hide Your face from my sins And blot out all my iniquities.

¹⁰Create in me a clean heart, O God, And renew a steadfast spirit within me. ¹¹Do not cast me away from Your presence And do not take Your Holy Spirit from me. ¹²Restore to me the joy of Your salvation And sustain me with a willing spirit. ¹³Then I will teach transgressors Your ways, And sinners will be converted to You.

[14]Deliver me from bloodguiltiness, O God, the God of my salvation; Then my tongue will joyfully sing of Your righteousness. [15]O Lord, open my lips, That my mouth may declare Your praise. [16]For You do not delight in sacrifice, otherwise I would give it; You are not pleased with burnt offering. [17]The sacrifices of God are a broken spirit; A broken and a contrite heart, O God, You will not despise.

[18]By Your favor do good to Zion; [n]Build the walls of Jerusalem. [19]Then You will delight in[j]righteous sacrifices, In burnt offering and whole burnt offering; Then young bulls will be offered on Your altar.

At the end of day one, I suggested writing a response to these two questions in our journals—what are your "first-impressions-all-over-again" of this Psalm? What is one hope you have for how God will speak to you and renew your spirit during this season of reflection?

Pause for a moment this day and review your answers to these questions. What stands out?

One word that stood out to me in my "first-impressions-again" reading is the word "behold" (found in verses five and six).

Here is a dictionary definition[2] of the word behold:

Behold: *to look at (something), to see (something) to perceive through sight or apprehension; to gaze upon.*

The synonyms suggest a deeper "seeing" than merely looking upon with our eyes. For example some of the synonyms include: appreciate, catch on to, decipher, seize and understand. Further, some of the related words include absorb, digest, penetrate and pierce.

The etymology of the word in English goes back to an Old English word meaning, "to keep," as reflected in the phrase, "to be beholden to."

These definitions jive with the translation from the original Hebrew as described in Strong's Concordance[3].

---

[2] Definitions from Merriam Webster, online version retrieved March 12, 2014, 8:33 AM at: http://www.merriam-webster.com/dictionary/behold

Strong further elaborates that this word (hen, in Hebrew) is *"mostly confined to calling attention to some fact upon which action is to be taken, or a conclusion based"*.

As we begin week two of this study together, please join me in this prayer:

"Lord, help me to pay attention so that I may behold what you have for me to see, absorb and digest through your words in Psalm 51. Give me eyes to see in such a way that I will truly catch on to and understand the depth and fullness of your message. Pierce me with your word; give me the courage to allow it to penetrate my heart and spirit. Show me the actions you desire for me to take as a result of beholding you on this day, and this week and throughout this season. Strengthen my desire to be beholden to you and only you."

Meditate for a few moments on the meanings and synonyms of the word "behold" and make a few notes in your journal. Listen to the praise song

"We Shall Behold Him" (sung by Sandi Patty) as you worship and reflect.

http://www.youtube.com/watch?v=3uXUm8-pSoM&feature=kp

---

[3] Strong's Concordance, online version, retrieved March 12, 2014, 8:44 AM at: http://biblehub.com/hebrew/2005.htm

Day 9 – Introduction to Theme 2

"Our Separation from God"
Read Verses 3, 4, 5
For I know my transgressions, And my sin is ever before me. 4 Against You, You only, I have sinned And done what is evil in Your sight, So that You are justified when You speak And blameless when You judge.

5 Behold, I was brought forth in iniquity, And in sin my mother conceived me.

It's a good thing we were immersed in God's holiness, unfailing lovingkindness and generous compassion last week because today we begin an entire week focused on the breadth and depth of our separation from God due to sin. It would be nearly impossible to plumb these depths without the secure knowledge that God's love endures forever and his mercies will never fail us.

As the week proceeds we will unpack these verses one-by-one, but let's begin today by examining a few overall impressions.

Evil – such a heavy word. That is one of my first thoughts upon reflecting on this passage. *"Ok, Lord, I know I have sinned, I continue to sin, I have lots of stuff I need to get straight with you on. But evil? Have I really done "evil in your sight"?* A few years ago a phrase was popularized to describe the perceived enemies of America—they were called "evil evil-doers." Am I, too, an "evil evil-doer?"

There are days when I am too complacent and too confident in my own "basic goodness." I recognize sin in myself, yet I do not accept or own the fact that it is "evil in your sight." I am reminded of a child, who, when confronted with doing something that he should not be doing will look up with that wide-eyed expression and say, "What? I didn't do anything." or at other times, "Why are you so mad over such a small thing?"

And yet, we as parents, or grandparents know that the seemingly small thing—a little lie, arguing with his mother, taking a toy from a sibling—these are not small things at all because it is through working on these seemingly small things that we develop the building blocks of character. When the child says, "I didn't do anything!" or "It's such a small thing!" I know he truly believes it. He doesn't see the error of his ways or the significance of a "small thing" in terms of the impact it can have on his whole life.

And so in that same way, when God uses a passage like this to call me on my evil ways, one of my first inclinations is to say, "What? I didn't do anything that bad. Why are you so mad?" I don't lump myself in with the "truly" evil ones in the world—the Hitlers, Osama bin Ladens or rapists, child abusers and murderers of the world. I'm not like *them*—right God?

In those moments I need to remember that even the small sins take me off the path of light and into the edge of darkness. They turn my feet away from God and in that respect they are evil in God's eyes. One of the dictionary definitions of evil is "causing ruin". God knows that when I allow the "small" or "lesser" sins to infiltrate my life, I am causing ruin in my own life.

When I think about it that way, I truly begin to feel the full weight and heaviness—the evil of my sins. I feel far from God and so unworthy of his love. How can God ever forgive me, the real me, the inner me with the heart that is at times manipulative and at times dishonest and at times lazy and at times prideful?

Do I get it and truly repent, or do I say, "Whatever, yeah, sorry, sorry" in a half-hearted way like children sometimes say to their parents?

Lord, during this time of reflection and prayer, I pray that you help me to understand and truly "get" the full weight of my sin, the fact that even if I am not a terrorist or murderer, I am still evil in your sight and that you are totally blameless when you judge me. Help me to recognize this at the deepest level so that I will have the broken and contrite heart that is needed for the full and complete cleansing and restoration you want for me. Amen.

A beautiful song for reflection today is "I Don't Deserve You" – listen to it as you make a few notes about the weightiness of sin in your own journal.
http://www.youtube.com/watch?v=Im5aoy5hKVA &feature=kp

Day 10 — Knowing

Read Verse 3

For I know my transgressions, And my sin is ever before me.

Today, let's focus on the first half of this verse. Do I really *know* my transgressions? I think I do, but have they become so comfortable, so familiar, so much a part of me and who I am that I don't even recognize them as sin anymore?

This question brings to mind an important concept I teach to foster and adoptive parents caring for children who have experienced trauma. Often these children have developed unhealthy or unsavory habits and the new parents want to break these habits quickly in their home. For example, many children hoard food in every pocket of their clothing, under their mattress and in dresser drawers. This can draw unwanted insects and rodents into the home to the dismay of many parents. Another example is a pre-teen girl who would wake up in the night needing the bathroom but could not bring herself to leave her room. She was awake and aware enough not to want to wet her bed, so she developed the habit of peeing in a mayonnaise jar and leaving it in a corner of her room. The stench alone was enough to disturb the adoptive parents, never mind other implications of this habit.

Anyone can understand why parents would not want these habits to continue. Yet, we have to learn not to take away these survival tools our children have developed without first learning why they were developed and helping the child to develop a new, safer, healthier habit to replace the old one. The child who hoards food is often responding to the painful

24

memory of unrelenting hunger or emotional neglect, while the child peeing in the jar had a history of sexual abuse.

To be clear, hoarding food or peeing in a jar are **not sins**. However, some children's tenacious hanging on to unhealthy habits even after the threat or trauma is removed is reminiscent of our own tenacity in hanging on to the unsavory sins we cling to—sinful habits we may have developed as part of our own response to coping with a broken and dangerous world. These deeply engrained sins in our lives also entice "rodents" to infest our lives and create a stench around our spirit as strong as a jar full or urine in the corner.

The child will eventually be ready to discard these habits when she feels safe, secure, loved and when she has opportunities to learn new ways of coping with reminders of past traumas.

Similarly, when we feel safe, secure and beloved by God and when we learn His new ways for us to cope with the hurts and wounds in our own lives, we will be better able to see our sins for what they are, to truly "know" our transgressions and begin the difficult work of shedding them.

My husband had some great insight on this verse when he said that he used to think that being a Christian meant that he couldn't be himself anymore, whereas over time he has learned that being a Christian means he can truly be his best self. I pray that God can use this time of prayer and fasting to show each of us how to be our best selves and not to accept second best in ourselves.

Will you pray with me, *"Lord help me to recognize my transgressions and not simply accept them as 'this is who I am.' Help me to turn them over to you and allow you to teach me new, and better, ways to cope with life's challenges and traumas. May I submit them to you and allow you to cleanse them and wash them away from me. Amen."*

Today's song for reflection is "Desperate" by the Christian rap artist Lacrae.
https://www.youtube.com/watch?v=c8IMvTYwXTw

Day 11 — Ever Before Me

Read Verse 3

For I know my transgressions, And my sin is ever before me.

Yesterday, we focused on knowing our sins, today, let's reflect on the second half of the verse: *"my sin is ever before me."* Even after I learn to *know* my sins, do I really *see* them *"ever before me?"*

In seeking to better understand this concept of sin being *"ever before me,"* I turn to Jeremiah 6:7 ~

"As a well keeps its waters fresh, So she keeps fresh her wickedness. Violence and destruction are heard in her; Sickness and wounds are ever before Me.

This passage, in which God is talking about the city of Jerusalem, creates a vivid word picture. I can instantly see neighborhoods in my own city of Philadelphia, neighborhoods that have been devastated and decimated by the ravages of poverty, violence, racism, addictions, injustice and abandonment. Children, and the adults who care for them, living in these neighborhoods are surrounded by violence, destruction, sickness and wounds. These blights are indeed, *"ever before"* them twenty-four hours a day, seven days a week.

In such an environment, is it any wonder that many find it nearly impossible to concentrate at school, to apply one's best self to a job, or even to show a tender moment of compassion to a neighbor?

In the context of this word picture, I turn my thoughts back to my own sin. I see that it is, indeed, *ever before me.* Like Jerusalem, I keep my sins fresh as well water. I freshen and re-freshen the supply with unfailing regularity. I drink from that tainted well and it fills my spirit with sickness and wounds.

You know how it is to be sick—the sickness truly is *"ever before"* you. When I am sick, my energy sags, my vision blurs, my hearing is dulled, my temples throb. In this depleted state, I am grumpy, short-tempered, not terribly loving. In this context, I find it nearly impossible to concentrate on daily tasks or to show tender moments of compassion to a child, a neighbor, a friend. My mind, my emotions and my spirit are consumed with a chorus of whining voices within me, throwing a pity-party for my poor sick self. In those moments, I desperately need a healing balm.

In the midst of that all-consuming sickness how refreshing it is when someone—my husband, a child or a friend—breaks through the fog and ministers to me in love. It may be as simple as a hand-crayoned get-well message from a toddler, or a steaming bowl of chicken noodle soup delivered by a friend. Often such small and simple gestures become balm with the power to snap me out of the sickness-infested spiritual fog and turn my heart back to Jesus. And when I do, even if the physical or emotional ailments linger my hope is renewed.

I am thankful for the people who have come into my life at just the right moment in a similar way to deliver the balm of spiritual "chicken noodle soup," piercing the dark fog of sin that is ever before me and reminding me of the hope I have in Jesus. I pray that I can be that soup-bearing balm-giver bringing both physical and emotional comfort as well as the life-giving hope of Jesus to those children and adults who live with the darkness of sin, violence and sickness *"ever before"* them.

As you reflect on this passage quietly listen to the song, "Balm in Gilead"
http://www.youtube.com/watch?v=BN9JALQRMbo
and write a few notes in your journal today.

Day 12 – You Alone

Read verse 4

"Against you, you only, have I sinned and done what is evil in your sight, so that you are proved right when you speak and justified when you judge."

"Against you, you only have I sinned." Hmmmm, is that really true? It seems to me that many times my sins hurt others—my husband, my kids, my colleagues at work, others in the church or community. And surely the sins of other people that I am most aware of are the ones that hurt me, or my kids. So how can it be *"against you (God) and you only that I have sinned?"*

A sports analogy comes to mind. If one player is messing up, it can ruin the game for the whole team. And so his mess-up is against the coach, the owner, the manager of the team. Sure it has an impact on him and the other players, but the bottom line is, it truly impacts the owner of the team the most. It prevents him from taking the team in the direction he wants it to go. Sometimes the whole game, and to some extent the whole season can come down to the result of one play—one small mistake by one player that changed the outcome.

I remember how stunned the city of Philadelphia was in 1993 when, while winning in Game four of the World Series, Joe Carter of the Blue Jays hit a bottom-of-the-ninth three-run home-run to not only win the game but the World Series. We learned this was the first time in the history of the World Series that a come-from-behind walk-off home run actually decided the outcome of the Series. One play. One pitch. One "mess-up" by the relief pitcher who received death threats after that game because serving up that home-run pitch was perceived by some fans to be a grievous error against the entire team and indeed the entire city of Philadelphia.

The analogy can be made for a business, family or any other organization. How often do we tell children that their behavior when out in public not only reflects on them, but also on the whole family, and most especially on us as the parents? We are all part of God's "organization" and in that sense, when we "mess up" (sin) it messes up his work and mission in the world. It brings to mind Matthew 18-5-7:

"And whoever receives one such child in My name receives Me; but whoever causes one of these little ones who believe in Me to stumble, it would be better for him to have a heavy millstone hung around his neck, and to be drowned in the depth of the sea. 7"Woe to the world because of its stumbling blocks! For it is inevitable that stumbling blocks come; but woe to that man through whom the stumbling block comes!

When I sin, I am creating a stumbling block along the path to God's kingdom and it is in that way that my sin is ultimately against him even more so than against the individual person I may have hurt in the process.

Lord, during this time of reflection and prayer, help me to recognize that every sin is a sin against you—whether the "secret" sins inside my heart, or sins that seem to be "just my problem" or those sins that hurt others. Help me to see every sin as a stumbling block I am laying in the path to your kingdom and give me the strength and the courage to refrain from sins so as not to be the one "through whom the stumbling block comes! Amen."

Listen to "You Alone" while reflecting and writing in your journal this day.

https://www.youtube.com/watch?v=jehFoSYiaSU

Day 13 – Proved Right

Read verse 4

"Against you, you only, have I sinned and done what is evil in your sight, so that you are proved right when you speak and blameless when you judge."

Today let's focus on the second half of this verse – *"you are proved right when you speak and blameless when you judge."*

There is something so deeply human about this passage in the words "you are proved right." God is the one who will be "proved right" but why does He have to be "proved?" He is already, always and eternally right. We have seen on earlier days in this study that God's love and compassion are unfailing and enduring. Surely this everlasting aspect of His character and his nature also apply to His judgments. So why does the psalmist feel the need to say that God will be "proved right?"

The same concept of being proved right, as written in the original Hebrew is found elsewhere in the Bible but none more powerfully than in Isaiah chapter forty-three. I urge you to read the entire chapter and then return to this reflection. The chapter is at once tender, full of compassion, powerful, full of God's holy righteousness and convicting. The concept of "proving one's case" is threaded throughout this chapter, and in verse ten God declares, *"YOU are my witnesses. . . so that you may know and believe me and understand that I am He."*

As the chapter continues, God eventually turns from making the case for his total all-consuming righteousness and rightness to the depth and breadth of the sins of His people—including you and me. In that context, we come to verse twenty-six which uses the same Hebrew term translated as "proved right" found here and in Psalm 51:

"Let us argue our case together; State your cause, that you may be proved right."

This need to prove something right and the picture it paints including witnesses and judges brings to mind a court hearing. But in another sense, it also brings to mind a sporting event, with the umpires or referees as the judges and the players and fans as the witnesses.

So to continue with the sports analogies used yesterday, consider being a fan at an exciting and important game—a game like the World Series Game Four described in yesterday's reflection. The umpires and referees in sporting events make many calls throughout the game. "Out!" "Safe!" "Foul!" "Penalty!"

Often the players and fans agree with these calls and the game moves smoothly along from one play to the next. But sometimes there is uproar. Players, coaches and fans are screaming, chanting, stomping their feet in anger when they feel an error in judgment has been made. In those situations we want the play reviewed. We want to look at the "instant replay" footage to re-consider the outcome.

Most of the time, even when instant replays are reviewed, the umpire or referee is "proved right." The review is not so much for the integrity of the umpire or referee but for the rest of us—the "witnesses"—the players on the field and the fans in the stands. We intently demand that our desire for "truth" and "justice" be satisfied and that the call is, in fact, wholly right.

Human umpires and referees sometimes err and are occasionally "proved wrong." Not so with our God. He will always be "proved right." So who does the proving? What is the "instant replay" in God's kingdom? This is where we come in. *"YOU are my witnesses"* God declares. When we live an upright life, when we acknowledge God in all of our ways, when we confess our sins not only to God but also to one another, we are the "instant replays" that will bear witness to God's eternal rightness and glory.

We are the witnesses who make it *"Clear in the eyes of the world"* that God is righteous, that He has not now nor has he ever "done us wrong." He is, indeed, in the words of one commentator, *"free from all charge of harshness or injustice."*[4]

Will you pray with me today— *"Lord, through the power of your Holy Spirit make my whole life glow with your light, so that I may indeed be one of your witnesses proving your righteousness and glory to the world? Make my life, truly, a prayer to you and a witness of your work in this world. Amen."*

Today is a great day to listen to Keith Green's "Make My Life a Prayer to You" while reflecting and writing in your journal.

http://www.youtube.com/watch?v=PNww8F6G9U8

---

[4] http://biblehub.com/commentaries/pulpit/psalms/51.htm

Day 14 – Invisible

Read verse 5

"Behold, I was brought forth in iniquity, And in sin my mother conceived me."

This is a challenging verse to grasp. Conceived in sin? How can this be so? Surely my parents were not in sin when they conceived me! They were married after all. Yet it is true, my sin begins at the beginning. I am one of the "all" in Romans 3:23, as were my parents: *"for ALL have sinned and fall short of the glory of God."* Spurgeon[5] phrases it this way: "I naturally lean to forbidden things."

Leviticus 5:2 is helpful in discerning this verse. *"Suppose you **unknowingly** touch something that is ceremonially unclean, such as the carcass of an unclean animal. When you realize what you have done, you must admit your defilement and your guilt"* (NLT) This demonstrates that beyond the concept of being "sinful by nature" is the concept that I can sin unknowingly.

This makes me think of my children and grandchildren. How many times (a day) do they do something that is upsetting, irritating or annoying to me—even if they do it unknowingly. If two children are playing and one accidently knocks the other child over, the second child is still hurt—the lack of intention on the part of the first child does not diminish the result for the second child.

I sin against God by my own irresponsibility and carelessness in addition to the times when I sin with intention.

---

[5] http://www.spurgeon.org/treasury/ps051.htm

In the second instance, there are two sins hand-in-hand—the sin of the heart (intention) and the sin of the action. Both require confession and cleansing.

This verse provides the perfect segue between this week's exploration of sin and next week's focus on the theme of cleansing found throughout Psalm 51.

When children play outside, getting dirty and muddy, they understand that they need to wash their hands before helping me make dinner. But if they washed their hands an hour ago and "didn't do anything" to get dirty in the meantime, they don't understand why I still want them to wash their hands before handling food. They show me hands that look clean and say, "Look, my hands are already clean, I don't need to wash them." And yet, I know about the germs in the air and on the many surfaces they have touched since the last time they washed. I know that even if they can't see dirt on their hands, they need to wash up before I am going to let them handle food!

My intentional sins, those I am consciously aware of, are as obvious as dirty hands after playing in the yard. The need for confession and cleansing is apparent. But my inherent sinful nature is more akin to the invisible dirtiness on the hands of children. The germs from the air that has attached to their skin and needs cleansing before they can handle food. My natural sin, the sin that has always been part of who I am, this too needs cleansing. It is not enough just to wash away the obvious dirt, but to also allow God to wash me so that the sinful nature that is part of my human condition can also be cleansed.

If I understand how important it is to wash "invisible" germs off of my hands before I handle food, how much more should I understand that I need to be cleansed by God of the "invisible" sins of my nature before I handle things much more important than food—such as my children and relationships.

Likewise, if washing my hands once in the morning is not sufficient to keep them clean enough all day to handle food, than one prayer in the morning is not sufficient to keep me clean enough to handle every precious thing God has in mind for me to handle throughout the day. Yet another reason to *"pray without ceasing."*

As we conclude our reflection on our second theme, let's pray, *"Lord help me to understand that even on a "good day" I am still a sinner, I am still in need of your cleansing, and renewal. My sinfulness is not just a master list of all my "bad acts" (like a spiritual rap sheet), but it is that part of my nature that "naturally leans toward forbidden things." Help me to recognize this and submit this part of myself to you so that I can be my best self, and you can shape me to lean toward the things you desire. Help me to adopt the discipline and habit of "praying without ceasing."Amen*

Listen to "Rejoice. Pray without Ceasing" while reflecting and writing notes in your journal today:

http://www.youtube.com/watch?v=RfMuideUf4c

Day 15 – Waiting

Read Psalm 51

We have completed the first two weeks in our study, focused on the themes of God's Holiness and the Our Separation from God. As we prepare our hearts for week three, which, beginning tomorrow, will focus on the theme, "Cleansing" let's take a moment today to go back and read the entire Psalm again.

Be gracious to me, O God, according to Your lovingkindness; According to the greatness of Your compassion blot out my transgressions. ² Wash me thoroughly from my iniquity And cleanse me from my sin. ³ For I know my transgressions, And my sin is ever before me. ⁴ Against You, You only, I have sinned And done what is evil in Your sight, So that You are justified when You speak And blameless when You judge.

⁵ Behold, I was brought forth in iniquity, And in sin my mother conceived me. ⁶ Behold, You desire truth in the innermost being, And in the hidden part You will make me know wisdom. ⁷ Purify me with hyssop, and I shall be clean; Wash me, and I shall be whiter than snow. ⁸ Make me to hear joy and gladness, Let the bones which You have broken rejoice. ⁹ Hide Your face from my sins And blot out all my iniquities.

¹⁰ Create in me a clean heart, O God, And renew a steadfast spirit within me. ¹¹ Do not cast me away from Your presence And do not take Your Holy Spirit from me. ¹² Restore to me the joy of Your salvation And sustain me with a willing spirit. ¹³ Then I will teach transgressors Your ways, And sinners will be converted to You.

14 Deliver me from bloodguiltiness, O God, the God of my salvation; Then my tongue will joyfully sing of Your righteousness. 15 O Lord, open my lips, That my mouth may declare Your praise. 16 For You do not delight in sacrifice, otherwise I would give it; You are not pleased with burnt offering. 17 The sacrifices of God are a broken spirit; A broken and a contrite heart, O God, You will not despise.

18 By Your favor do good to Zion; [n]Build the walls of Jerusalem. 19 Then You will delight in]righteous sacrifices, In burnt offering and whole burnt offering; Then young bulls will be offered on Your altar.

At the end of day one, I suggested writing a response to these two questions in our journals—what are your "first-impressions-all-over-again" of this Psalm? What is one hope you have for how God will speak to you and renew your spirit during this season of reflection?

In response to those questions, at the end of the first week, we focused on the word "Behold" and prayed to both see deeply and to be beholden to God during this season. Today, as we again seek to have our spirits renewed, I'd like to focus on the concept of waiting. Both Lent and Advent are seasons of waiting as we prepare our hearts to fully absorb and accept God's amazing grace and gifts to us in both the incarnation and the resurrection.

Waiting can be hard to do. I was in a book group meeting recently and the book we were discussing was about a family who encountered a very dangerous situation. One of the group members confessed, *"Whenever I am reading a book where people might die, I have to read the last chapter right away— I can't wait to find out if they are going to live or die."* Many of us could relate. Waiting can be stressful.

There are many, many passages throughout both the Old and New Testaments about the concept of waiting for and waiting on the Lord. One of my favorites is found in Psalms 37:7, which I have quoted here in three different versions so we can really grasp the richness of this idea of waiting:

"Rest in the Lord and wait patiently for Him Psalm 37:7 (NASB)

"Be silent before the LORD and wait expectantly for Him" (Holman)

"Be still in the presence of the Lord, and wait patiently for him to act." (NLT)

Rest. Be silent. Be still. I am not fidgety by nature. I can sit still. But stilling my mind is another story. Even when I pray, or meditate, my thoughts fly off in a hundred directions. Being still is not for slackers. It is hard work! I Love the way Spurgeon describes it:

"Rest in the Lord." This fifth is a most divine precept, and requires much grace to carry it out. To hush the spirit, to be silent before the Lord, to wait in holy patience[6]

Wait expectantly. Wait in holy patience. Wait and see what the Lord will do. In me. In my loved ones. In my community. In the world.

Today, instead of sharing a prayer filled with words, I invite you to rest. Be silent. Be still. Wait in holy patience, expectantly, for the Lord.

"The LORD is good to those who wait for Him, To the person who seeks Him." Lamentations 3:25

Be Still and Know:

http://www.youtube.com/watch?v=BgaHaioAjyg

---

[6] Commentary from Spurgeon's Treasury of David as found on Bible-Hub, retrieved March 21, 2014 8:19 AM http://biblehub.com/psalms/37-7.htm

Day 16 – Introduction to Theme 3

"Cleansing"

Read Verses 2, 7, 9 and 10

2: Wash me thoroughly from my iniquity And cleanse me from my sin.

7: Purify me with hyssop, and I shall be clean; Wash me, and I shall be whiter than snow.

9 Hide Your face from my sins And blot out all my iniquities.

10: Create in me a clean heart, O God, And renew a steadfast spirit within me.

Phew—week two might have been a little tough to get through—a whole week focused on the depth of our sinful selves and the resulting separation from God. It is with a sense of relief and hopefulness that we can turn to week three and focus on the theme of God's Cleansing. God is the one who can cleanse us from that sin we are so deeply mired in! Hallelujah!

Even so, I can't help but wonder—is there enough soap even in God's hands to wash away all of that and truly cleanse me? Is that why I cannot feel as close to God as I want, because of the evil that still stubbornly sticks to my heart? Am I like many of the coffee mugs in our kitchen—scrubbed clean on the outside, but even after several times through the dishwasher, some of the coffee stains remain stubbornly refusing to come off?

How will I ever get truly clean? I need Jesus for that.

I believe the cleansing begins with spiritual cleansing, and that is clearly described throughout this Psalm. But I also believe it refers to mental, emotional and physical cleansing. Which is why it's so great to reflect on this cleansing during Lent or at the beginning of spring. It gives us the chance to do a complete and thorough "spring cleaning" and "de-tox" for the body, mind and soul.

When I clean my room or desk, I rarely (if ever) "go all the way" to truly unclutter it. I clear stuff off the visible spaces, load things into boxes, throw out a lot of garbage and then consider it a job well done. Those boxes go into a closet and I don't completely sort and "unclutter" them. Meanwhile, I keep some sense of order for a while and then slowly allow the clutter to return. When I first see the clutter returning, I begin to tackle it, picking up a few days worth of stuff, getting it back to the level of order I had created. But eventually, the clutter takes over and I am back at square one. I am then overwhelmed and defeated, and so doing even a few small steps seems impossible. Can you relate to that?

This week, as we focus on cleansing, let us consider how to fully "de-clutter" our inner-selves. Spiritually, mentally, physically and emotionally, down to the deepest parts, not leaving a few "boxes" behind for later sorting. Let's consider how to strengthen our resolve to maintain the new, clean, well-ordered selves, while recognizing that we will not always be perfect. Together let's develop the keen eye that will help us to recognize when clutter is beginning to accumulate in our lives again so we can immediately take action to clean up and restore order.

No matter how much spiritual, mental, physical or emotional clutter surrounds us, I pray that each of us will have the wisdom, strength and courage to actually start somewhere, even with small steps, picking up one or two things, not waiting until we have the strength, energy or time to do the whole thing.

Will you pray with me that by the end of this seasoning of prayer and reflection we will feel truly cleansed in all respects and will be on the road to a lifestyle that will keep us cleaner and healthier in all ways? From our head to our heart, our nose to our toes, let's prepare to be washed thoroughly. Into the bath we go!

As you reflect on our theme for this week and jot a few notes in your journal, listen to the powerful gospel song, "Wade in the Water"

http://www.youtube.com/watch?v=HQwr-DIs_VQ

Day 17 – Wash Me!

Read Verse 2

"Wash me thoroughly from my iniquity And cleanse me from my sin."

Read also Jeremiah 2:22 *"Although you wash yourself with soap and use an abundance of cleansing powder, the stain of your guilt is still before me," declares the Sovereign LORD"* (NIV)

The most immediate thing that struck me when I reflected on these verses is that we need God to wash us—I need God to wash me. It is not enough to do it ourselves because even an "abundance of soap" is not enough to cleanse us from our sins when we try to do it ourselves.

These reflections on washing make me think of children who like to wash up in the kitchen sink, or take a bath. Sometimes they use "an abundance of soap." Bubbles and suds everywhere! Sometimes they love the bath—laughing and squealing with delight as they play and splash in it. Sometimes they resist our efforts to wash them—proudly declaring that they can do it themselves.

Their washing is not totally in vain. They do get cleaner than they were before. The most obvious dirt sloughs off in the soapy water and by virtue of their efforts. They do not emerge from the bath as dirty as they went in.

This is like me with God, trying to "get myself clean" with my own efforts. With some prayer, reading the confession in church with others, trying to refrain from bad habits and sinful activities and turning towards more positive activities. It is not totally in vain. It is good to shake loose the "dirt" of laziness or anger, bitterness or judgment, mindlessness or wastefulness. I believe that just as we as parents or grandparents smile and are pleased with the efforts of our children to get themselves clean, so God too is able to smile at our efforts to cleanse ourselves.

And yet, it is not enough. It is not enough to let an infant or toddler "do it myself" or they will never be clean. In the realm of eternity, we are but babes or at best toddlers in God's kingdom. It is not enough for us to try to clean ourselves, as the Jeremiah passage demonstrates; even when we use "an abundance of soap" the stain of our guilt is still before him.

When we move from playtime to serious cleaning time with an infant or small child, the laughter sometimes turns to tears. The child does not like it so much when we scrub the places where the dirt is really ground in. She doesn't like us getting behind the ears.

We also have to get the places that are hard for the child to reach herself—the back and butt for example. This is no longer play but serious business and so important. The child may complain, yell, cry and squirm to get away, but the good parent will patiently and persistently continue to wash the child until the child is thoroughly clean.

Are you ready to join me in saying to God, *"My playtime in the bath is over, come and wash me. Get behind my ears, get all the hard to reach places. Help me to not squirm away from Your washing. Rather give me the courage to allow You to get to all the hard places, the stained places, and the hidden places where the dirt and crud has accumulated. Wash away all of my iniquities and cleanse me thoroughly even though I may not like it!"*

As we reflect and write in our journals today, let's listen to "What Can Wash Away my Sin". This version, sung by a child is particularly appropriate to go with our reflection today: **http://www.youtube.com/watch?v=sLHMKKAJF-o**

Day 18 – Scrub me!

Read Verse 7

Purify me with hyssop, and I shall be clean; Wash me, and I shall be whiter than snow.

Yesterday, we jumped into the spiritual bubble bath and started getting cleansed by playing and splashing. We quickly recognized that even with an "abundance of soap" we could not thoroughly cleanse ourselves, so we ended by turning the washcloth and soap over to God for the more serious cleansing even in hard-to-reach places.

Getting thoroughly clean is going to take some serious scrubbing. How does God scrub us? Hyssop is mentioned in this verse and elsewhere in the Bible where thorough cleansing is required (see Exodus 12:22 and Numbers 19:17-19 for example). Carefully studying the uses of hyssop in the Bible, including the fact that hyssop was used during the crucifixion to provide vinegar to Jesus when he was thirsty, demonstrates that it had both literal and symbolic significance. Both literally and figuratively, hyssop provides deep cleansing and purification, and foreshadows of true cleansing that only comes by the blood of Jesus.

So—what is hyssop anyway?

The plant translated as "hyssop" in these passages is also known as ezov, a plant of the marjoram, thyme and mint family, or capers. While today we think of these plants as useful in cooking, let's take a moment to consider the properties that make them useful for deep spiritual scrubbing and cleansing.

There are four interesting and relevant characteristics of the plants in the family translated biblically as hyssop.

First, these plants are hardy and plentiful—they grow nearly anywhere, requiring little in the way of soil, light or water as other plants do. They grow on walls and in crevices. This tells me that God wants us to know that His deep spiritual cleansing is always readily available to us. Isn't it comforting to know that no matter what wall we are up against or how deep and dark the crevices of sin we fall into, there is nowhere we can go where God's cleansing cannot reach us? (See Romans 8:38-39)

Second the hyssop families of plants typically have long, stiff and prickly stems. What could be better for scrubbing especially in the hard-to-reach places? It is long—like those long-handled back-scrubbers we can buy today in a bath and body shop. It is strong (stiff) so it will hold up to the strong pressure required when scrubbing a particularly stubborn stain. And it is prickly—like steel wool it has the ability to get even the toughest stains out. How awesome is it that God provides a scrubbing tool that is so durable and effective! Although of course the application of such a stiff and prickly implement on my tender skin is likely to be a little uncomfortable. Getting scrubbed clean may not always be pleasant.

Third, these plants are known to have cleansing and healing properties. In fact, some of the plants in this family have anti-viral properties that not only clean and disinfect, but also help protect the spreading of germs. In addition, today, the ezov plant is marketed for its ability to provide "emotional balance." God thinks of everything, doesn't he? He knows we not only need specific sins washed away, but also we need to be protected against the spread of both the sin and its consequences. Not unlike the concept behind the development of modern "anti-bacterial" soaps, God's soap is the real deal—no side effects, no need for an FDA warning label. And isn't it true that when we experience this deep cleansing we also feel "emotionally balanced" and restored?

Finally my favorite property—these plants are all aromatic—they smell good! Isn't that one of the joys of getting truly clean—all the stench of dirt, filth and even body odors are washed away and we emerge from the bath smelling sweet and fresh. We all want cleaning products that not only cleanse but also leave a pleasing odor. Have you seen those Febreze commercials? These products are new and yet thousands of years ago our God was already offering us the opportunity not only to be clean but to smell clean too!

I think of hyssop now every time I shower. I use a long handled body-scrubber with a loofah sponge on the end and it reminds me of the deep physical, emotional and spiritual scrubbing I have access to with God's hyssop. As we each reflect on today's passage and write in our journal, let's listen to Point of Grace, Wash Me Away:

http://www.youtube.com/watch?v=c7pTkHuyxEI

Day 19 – Blotted Out!

Read Verse 9

Hide Your face from my sins And blot out all my iniquities.

So far this week, we splashed around playfully in a bubble bath with an "abundance of soap," and then succumbed to the serious scrubbing needed to reach the hard and hidden places, aided by a stalk of hyssop and God's strong, guiding hand. We emerged from that deep cleansing fresh, clean and sweet-smelling.

Ahhhhhhh . . . . . isn't it great?

But wait! Now we are standing on the bath mat, dripping wet and still naked!

Have you ever noticed that as children get to be about seven or eight years old they are not shy about their bodies while they are still in the tub, but as soon as they step out, naked, they say, "Don't look!" and then they quickly want to be wrapped with a towel?

This is where we find ourselves today, standing clean, but naked, in the presence of our Lord. *"Hide your face from my sins!"* we cry, "Don't look!" We know we've been washed, yes, even scrubbed with hyssop, and yet we are still feeling a little vulnerable as we see that dirty-sin water swirling around on the bottom of the tub, heading for the drain.

And in that vulnerable moment, God is so very gracious to us. He hands us a thick, absorbent, fluffy towel and "blot's out" all the bath water that still clings to us.

In a thesaurus, the phrase "blot out" has some interesting synonyms. Words and phrases like "rub out," "wipe out," and

46

"erase" are compatible with the job our towel is doing for us as we step out of the bath.

But then it gets deeper. Some of the other synonyms are more intense, such as "decimate," "demolish," "obliterate." Getting the picture? After this "blotting out" takes place there is nothing left. Nothing. Whatever was there has been "finished off," "extinguished" and "exterminated."

Gone.

Finally, some of the synonyms evoke a legal act. To blot out also means to "quash," "expunge," and "annul." To make it as if it never happened.

Colossians Chapter two is an incredible testimony to our new life in Christ. We are exhorted that as we have received Christ, now we are to walk in Him. And as this chapter continues, we come upon verses thirteen and fourteen:

13 *You were dead because of your sins and because your sinful nature was not yet cut away. Then God made you alive with Christ, for he forgave all our sins.* **14** *He canceled the record of the charges against us and took it away by nailing it to the cross. (NLT)*

"He cancelled the record of the charges against us." In other words, he quashed, expunged and annulled them. In the King James version, verse fourteen begins: *"Blotting out the handwriting of ordinances that was against us . . ." (KJV).*

Knowing our deep need for cleansing, God gives us an opportunity to wash ourselves through prayer and confession. Recognizing that even an abundance of soap does not get us thoroughly clean, He then provides the implements necessary for a deep scrubbing—hyssop and the Blood of the cross. But even after that, He does the most amazing and generous thing of all. He doesn't leave us standing naked in the swirl of dirty water.

He blots us dry with His towel, the towel that not only absorbs but obliterates every last speck of sin and grime. Nothing is left behind. When we emerge from God's cleansing, we are not just clean and smelling fresh, we are completely made new. It is as if the sin never happened. Expunged.

There is no ring around this tub. All the dirt is gone.

Will you take a moment and thank God with me today? *"Dear Lord, thank you for your cleansing. Thank you for scrubbing me clean even in the deep and hard to reach places. And most of all, thank you for completely cancelling and eradicating every trace of dirt, grime and sinfulness from my life. This is too much for me to fathom, so I just come to you to rest in gratitude and faith, snuggled in my fluffy towel, feeling cleansed and loved from my nose to my toes. Thank you Lord God. Amen."*

Listen to this instrumental version of "My Sins are Blotted Out, I Know!" as you write a few reflections in your journal today.

http://www.youtube.com/watch?v=xW2YzX1otIM

Day 20 – New Heart

Read Verse 10

Create in me a clean heart, O God, And renew a steadfast spirit within me.

We will end week three by spending two days on this one powerful verse. Today, we will focus on the first phrase, "Create in me a clean heart, O God," and tomorrow we will turn to "renew a steadfast spirit within me."

If we've accepted the cleansing, the scrubbing, the purifying even with hyssop and blood that we've learned about over the past few days, we can envision ourselves today being pristine, wholly, squeaky clean, like a newborn baby fresh from the bath. Every last vestige and trace of sin has been blotted out.

So why isn't David ready to move on from this topic of cleansing?

He has one more important request of God – a *new heart*. Yes, the verse asks for a clean heart, and surely David wants this new heart to be clean. But notice the verb he chooses: "create." *"Create in me a clean heart, O God,"* suggests that he is asking not only for a clean heart but also for a *new* heart. To create means, *"to cause to come into being,"* and *"to evolve from one's own thought or imagination."*

David is not asking God to scrub his old heart, not even with hyssop. As this forgiven, purified, thoroughly cleansed person standing before his Lord, David is asking for a fresh, *new* heart, brought into being by God, and only by God, evolving from His thoughts and His imagination.

David knows that it was his heart that got him into trouble before. The unclean yearnings of his heart were too hard for his spirit, mind and body to resist and off he ventured into the deep, dark netherworld of sin that is called nothing short of evil in this Psalm. So now that he has submitted to God's cleansing, he desperately wants a new heart to help him sustain this newfound freedom from sin.

I believe God wants each of us to have a *new heart* today. A clean heart to be sure, but also a *new* heart.

I have been deeply disturbed in recent years as Christians in our communities and our world have been so bitterly divided on issues of politics, social justice and morality that one of my favorite Sunday school songs—"They'll know we are Christians by our Love"—has become a quaint relic of the past rather than a reality of the present.

I know and love Christian people who stand on completely opposite sides of such issues as gay marriage, foreign policy and who to vote for in local or Presidential elections. I am not talking about crazy people on the lunatic fringe—but sincere thoughtful people for whom their faith is the anchor and core of their very lives. They have studied scripture and researched the issues, prayed and fasted. And come to very different conclusions. I myself often find myself on different sides of some of these very issues than many of my brothers and sisters in Christ. I know that each of them loves the Lord their God with their whole heart, soul, mind and strength, as do I.

But do we always demonstrate what it means to love our neighbors as ourselves?

As I pondered what it would mean to have a *new* clean heart, God drew me to two other treasured passages of scripture (emphasis added):

But the Lord said to Samuel, "Don't judge by his appearance or height, for I have rejected him. The Lord doesn't see things the way you see them. People judge by outward appearance, but **the Lord looks at the heart**.*" (I Samuel 16:7, NLT) and*

6 So the apostles and elders met together to resolve this issue. 7 At the meeting, after a long discussion, Peter stood and addressed them as follows: "Brothers, you all know that

*God chose me from among you some time ago to preach to the Gentiles so that they could hear the Good News and believe. **8 God knows people's hearts**, and he confirmed that he accepts Gentiles by giving them the Holy Spirit, just as he did to us. **9** He made no distinction between us and them, for **he cleansed their hearts through faith**. **10** So why are you now challenging God by burdening the Gentile believers with a yoke that neither we nor our ancestors were able to bear? **11** We believe that we are all saved the same way, by the undeserved grace of the Lord Jesus." (Acts 15:6-11 NLT)*

It is not up to me, or any of us, to burden others with a yoke that "neither we nor our ancestors were able to bear." We need to trust that our God sees their heart, knows their heart and cleanses their heart just as he does with our own.

Our prayer today is simple, *"Create in me a new heart, O God. Cause it to come into being from Your thoughts and imagination, Your thoughts that are too high and lofty for me to understand. Create this new, clean heart in me today, and may it ever be new, day after day, O God, I pray. Amen."*

As you listen to "They'll Know We Are Christians By Our Love," reflect on the ways you can demonstrate your new heart by the way you show God's love to others.

http://www.youtube.com/watch?v=qrOywJnLj7Y

Day 21 – Steadfast

Read Verse 10

Create in me a clean heart, O God, And renew a steadfast spirit within me.

"Renew a steadfast spirit within me." Steadfast. Such a *solid* word, isn't it?

Of the many places this word and concept are found in scripture, here are two that especially speak to our theme today:

*"Therefore, my beloved brothers, be **steadfast**, immovable, always abounding in the Lord's work, because you know that your labor is not in vain in the Lord." I Corinthians 15:58 NASB*

*"This hope we have as an anchor of the soul, a hope both sure and **steadfast** and entering into that which is within the veil." Hebrews 6:19 NASB*

My grandfather was steadfast. He was solid. Immovable. Always abounding in the Lord's work. He demonstrated this especially in his approach to gardening. Being a gardener in Vermont is no easy task. The growing season is short and often the weather conspires against your best efforts. Yet, day after day, he was out there—steadfast in his work, knowing his labor was not in vain. There was no greater joy in my childhood than eating a ripe tomato from his garden, juices dripping luxuriantly down my chin, kissed by the sun while my grandfather, smiling, sat on the porch and quietly ate a tomato of his own.

Being steadfast and immovable requires great patience.

Today is the halfway mark in our six-week study of this Psalm and I don't know about you, but for me, this is the day when I recognize the need for patience to allow God to work in my life, and the lives of those I care about. It can be easy to succumb to the fear that my labor is in vain if I don't see results *now*.

I need to give God time to wash me, create a new, clean heart within me and endow me with a steadfast spirit before I am ready for the "and then" part of this Psalm. But I am impatient. I want it all and I want it now. I didn't want to spend a whole week last week reflecting on my sin. I just wanted to say confession and be done with it, moving on to being quickly cleansed, then receiving the inner truth, wisdom, renewed joy and opportunities to make a difference promised later in the Psalm.

I move too fast. My brain races ahead. I want assurances that my labor is not in vain. Reflecting on just one verse of the Psalm each day is hard for me yet also necessary to slow me down and help me to be patient. I need to take the time to reflect on each one of these verses and give God the opportunity to work in me and not expect the answers, the results, the fulfillment of the entire Psalm in just one day or even a couple of weeks.

I need to be steadfast.

Yet, even as I sit here and pray for patience, my mind races ahead craving whatever comes next. Can you relate to this?

"The hope we have as an anchor of the soul, a hope both sure and steadfast . . . " Hope that is not fleeting. Hope that is not fickle. Hope that doesn't depend on the weather, emotions, opinions of others, the money in my bank account or my appearance. Hope that is solid and endures.

This, then, is the end result of our week of cleansing. An opportunity to drop anchor. To fortify our secure foundation. To appreciate and understand and absorb what it means to be steadfast. To be solid. Immovable.

"Slow me down Lord, slow each of us down. Help us to savor every bite of this feast from your Word just as I savored those July tomatoes from my grandfather's garden. Let us be steadfast. Amen."

Make this song your prayer today as you reflect and write in your journal – "Lord find me steadfast, immovable."

https://www.youtube.com/watch?v=9pyT-Ujin9Q

Day 22 – Nourish Me!

Read Psalm 51

We have completed half of our study! We've reflected upon the themes of God's Holiness, Our Separation from God and God's perfect Cleansing. Tomorrow, we will begin the fourth week of our study by focusing on the theme "Truth in the Inner Being." As we have done in each of the previous weeks, let's begin by once again reading the entire Psalm:

Be gracious to me, O God, according to Your lovingkindness; According to the greatness of Your compassion blot out my transgressions. ²Wash me thoroughly from my iniquity And cleanse me from my sin. ³For I know my transgressions, And my sin is ever before me. ⁴Against You, You only, I have sinned And done what is evil in Your sight, So that You are justified when You speak And blameless when You judge.

⁵Behold, I was brought forth in iniquity, And in sin my mother conceived me. ⁶Behold, You desire truth in the innermost being, And in the hidden part You will make me know wisdom. ⁷Purify me with hyssop, and I shall be clean; Wash me, and I shall be whiter than snow. ⁸Make me to hear joy and gladness, Let the bones which You have broken rejoice. ⁹Hide Your face from my sins And blot out all my iniquities.

¹⁰Create in me a clean heart, O God, And renew a steadfast spirit within me. ¹¹Do not cast me away from Your presence And do not take Your Holy Spirit from me. ¹²Restore to me the joy of Your salvation And sustain me with a willing spirit. ¹³Then I will teach transgressors Your ways, And sinners will be converted to You.

14 Deliver me from bloodguiltiness, O God, the God of my salvation; Then my tongue will joyfully sing of Your righteousness. 15 O Lord, open my lips, That my mouth may declare Your praise. 16 For You do not delight in sacrifice, otherwise I would give it; You are not pleased with burnt offering. 17 The sacrifices of God are a broken spirit; A broken and a contrite heart, O God, You will not despise.

18 By Your favor do good to Zion; [n]Build the walls of Jerusalem. 19 Then You will delight in[j]righteous sacrifices, In burnt offering and whole burnt offering; Then young bulls will be offered on Your altar.

We ended week three of our study with this prayer, *"Lord, Help us to savor every bite of this feast from your Word."* This deep immersion into Psalm 51 is a bit like a feast, isn't it? As we prepare to begin week four, let's consider how God uses His word to feed and nourish us.

My husband and I did a study of Psalm 51 together during Lent in 2009 while our son Dylan was still alive. Dylan was one of our children who received his nourishment through tube feedings. He could not sit down at the table and eat with the rest of us, nor grab a snack on the run. He had to receive his nourishment slowly, through a constant supply of formula dripping into his body so that his digestive system could absorb and process it slowly. Each morning, while we studied the Word, Hector would pause for a moment to feed Dylan.

Watching Hector feed Dylan in this way, with Psalm 51 open on my lap, struck me as a beautiful example of how God desires to nourish us with his spiritual truth and wisdom. Not with a quick meal that we grab via the drive-through window of a fast-food restaurant while we are going about the "busy-ness" of our day. Nor through an occasional giant feast where we sit down and gorge ourselves on all kinds of food until we are stuffed to the gills and can barely move.

No, God knows that we need to receive His truth and wisdom in a slow, but steady, constant drip, so that we can absorb it, comprehend it and allow it to go all the way down to our "inmost parts".

The occasional fast food meal of a quick Bible verse and prayer, and the occasional spiritual feasts of full-day retreats, revivals or lengthy uninterrupted prayer are not bad things—in fact they add depth and dimension to our lives. But to truly gain the kind of inner truth and wisdom spoken of in this Psalm requires the slow, gentle, non-spectacular drip, drip, drip of a tube feeding—like the "blessed" one of Psalm 1: *"But his delight is in the law of the LORD, And in His law he meditates day and night."*

Today, consider how God is using His Word in this season to nourish you. Revisit your response to the question asked at the beginning of the study - What is one hope you have for how God will speak to you and renew your spirit during this season of reflection? As we continue to feast on His word, will you allow it to drip, drip; drip into your very being—*"day and night?"*

Today's hymn for reflection, "I Will Delight" **https://www.youtube.com/watch?v=sxIHYOq2IpE**

Day 23 – Introduction to Theme 4

"Truth in the Inner Being "

Read Verses 6, 16-17

Behold, You desire truth in the innermost being, And in the hidden part You will make me know wisdom.

16 For You do not delight in sacrifice, otherwise I would give it; You are not pleased with burnt offering. 17 The sacrifices of God are a broken spirit; A broken and a contrite heart, O God, You will not despise.

I believe that God wants us to hear His voice and know His truth and wisdom "down to our toes" in the deepest parts of our hearts and souls. This week, we will explore the meanings of "truth," "wisdom," and our "inner being." We are prepared and ready for this because we have spent the prior three weeks reflecting on God's holiness and our sin and then allowing ourselves to be thoroughly cleansed and receptive to the new, clean heart and steadfast spirit God desires to give us.

There is one more step in our preparation for truth and wisdom in our inner being. We need to be sure we are fully present and tuned in to hear God's voice. When I teach social workers, teachers and parents about caring for children who have experienced trauma, these are two of the most important concepts—being present and tuning in. While these are important skills in any relationship, they are even more important for vulnerable children who have had to shield their little hearts and spirits for survival and protection. They are not accustomed to having anyone truly "tune-in" to them or even to simply be present with them.

These two concepts are similar yet different. Being present is how we give of ourselves, and being tuned-in is how we receive from the other person in the relationship. When we are both present and tuned-in the communication flows freely in two directions, in the trauma world this is called, "serve and return" and it is similar to a tennis match or a ballet.

Being present means more than merely showing up, although that is a good start. Being present—to a child, to our spouse, friend or to God—has to do with how we *show* that we are engaged and able to listen not only with our ears but also with our hearts. Do we give eye contact? Stop other things that we are doing that may be distracting? Ask reflective questions that demonstrate active listening?

Being tuned-in means using all of our senses to absorb the fullness of the message the other person—or our God—intends to communicate. In human relationships, this means paying attention to eye contact, body language, and voice tone, not just the actual words that are spoken.

But what does being tuned-in mean when it comes to hearing God's voice and spirit in our life?

What comes to mind is listening to a radio. Sometimes the radio is on in the background but I'm not listening, I'm not tuned in, I don't hear what is being said. At those times, I need to silence my own thoughts enough to listen and reflect upon what I am hearing. At other times, God's voice is being broadcast—it is "on air" but I don't even have my radio turned on, or if it is on, I am not tuned into the right station. It may be set on static (the *noise* of the world) or perhaps another station (the *wisdom* of the world). I'm listening, but not hearing what God wants me to hear because I'm not tuned in to the right station.

Will you join me in praying that this week we will learn to be both present and tuned-in to God so that we can begin to experience truth and wisdom in our inner being? As you pray, reflect and write in your journal, tune in to this worship song:

I Will Listen, Twila Paris:
https://www.youtube.com/watch?v=wUnk1td2sQU

Day 24 – Truth

Read Verse 6

Behold, You desire truth in the innermost being,And in the hidden part You will make me know wisdom.

Today, we begin plumbing the depths of this gem of a verse. First, we'll explore the concept of "truth." What is the truth that God desires? The same word shows up in Psalm 15:1-2 and it is combined with the word "integrity:"

O Lord, who may abide in Your tent? Who may dwell on Your holy hill? He who walks with integrity, and works righteousness, And speaks truth in his heart. (NASB)

Taken together, these verses show me that God wants me to speak truth in my *own heart*—tell the truth even to myself. Integrity involves being transparent—the inner self and the outer self are indistinguishable. Tell the truth to myself.

This sounds simple and yet is profound.

How often do I justify things *to myself?* Both the times when I justify not doing what I should be doing, as well as when I justify doing what I should not do. God wants me to walk with integrity *even in the hidden parts.*

These questions and thoughts always make me think of Rebekah. She was cunning, conniving and manipulative as she tried to ensure that the "right" son received the father's blessing. (Genesis 27) And yet, she justified all of her actions *to herself.* To me, it seems as though she thought God had gotten the birth order wrong and needed her help in straightening things out.

She had stepped far away from the path of integrity. She lost her footing when she stopped speaking the truth *to her own heart.* Oh how I can relate to Rebekah! So many times I see things in the lives of people I care about—things that seem wrong, a mess or just off-kilter. I think I know what God must really want and so I decide He just needs a little help from me. I want to micro-manage things so they turn out exactly "right."

But God doesn't desire my micro-managing manipulation. He desires the integrity that comes from telling the truth to my own heart. Gaining this truth, this integrity is what is meant by sanctification. Let's take a look at John 17:17-19:

17 Sanctify them in the truth; Your word is truth. 18 As You sent Me into the world, I also have sent them into the world. 19 For their sakes I sanctify Myself, that they themselves also may be sanctified in truth.

Sanctify them in truth, Jesus prays—for us. Sanctification is the process of becoming more holy, more God-like in our very character and being. Developing God's integrity.

This makes me think of the process of an actor learning a part. Any decent actor can pick up a script and even on the very first reading give the listener some sense of the character—some depth, emotional quality, and nuance.

However, no actor can fully inhabit the character he or she is assigned to play on the first read-through. In interview after interview with actors, they talk about the process of truly becoming the character. The words of the script have to get deep down inside of them and they have to fully live and breathe their character. Practice helps, yet even after much practice multiple "takes" are required to get it right. Props, costume, and make-up all help. Surrounding himself with the other characters and the proper environment to set the mood and tone also help the actor to become one with his character.

Sanctification is somewhat like this, but at a deeper level. The "character" we are trying to become one with is no less than the God of the entire universe, and the "play" is not just for a run at the local theatre or even on Broadway, but for all of eternity.

How do we *become one* with and fully inhabit the character of the most high God?

By speaking the truth in our own hearts and then walking in integrity. Let's reflect on that a bit today, and write our reflections in our journals while listening to "Blest are the Pure in Heart"

https://www.youtube.com/watch?v=OMYVdGjUC2c

Day 25 – Wisdom

Read Verse 6

Behold, You desire truth in the innermost being, And in the hidden part You will make me know wisdom.

There is nothing quite like the beginning of a new school year. Children are excited to go back to school, see the friends they haven't seen over the summer, wear new clothes and take a measure of their new teacher. Going to the local shoe store with my mom and sisters a week before the start of school and getting my new pair of saddle shoes (until I graduated to penny loafers) is one of my favorite childhood memories!

When we first became parents of school-age children, we continued the tradition of buying new clothes and shoes for the first day of school. But we augmented it with a new tradition—for the first 31 days of the school year we read one Proverb each night at the dinner table. The Book of Proverbs contains so many nuggets of wisdom, we believed this annual repetition created a firm foundation for our children and ourselves as we thought about the true goal of schooling and education, as outlined in verses 1-7 of Proverbs 1 (NLT):

1 These are the proverbs of Solomon, David's son, king of Israel.

2 Their purpose is to teach people wisdom and discipline, to help them understand the insights of the wise.

3 Their purpose is to teach people to live disciplined and successful lives, to help them do what is right, just, and fair.

4 These proverbs will give insight to the simple, knowledge and discernment to the young.

5 Let the wise listen to these proverbs and become even wiser.   Let those with understanding receive guidance

6 by exploring the meaning in these proverbs and parables,   the words of the wise and their riddles.

7 Fear of the Lord is the foundation of true knowledge,   but fools despise wisdom and discipline.

When reading through the entire book of Proverbs, as well as doing a word-study throughout the Bible on the word "wisdom," we learn several things about wisdom:

1. You aren't born with wisdom-it must be **acquired** (Job 28, Proverbs 4)

2. Wisdom can be **taught and learned** (Proverbs 1:2)

3. Wisdom can be **increased** (Ecclesiastes 1)

4. Wisdom can also be **lost** (Job 39)

5. Wisdom is more **valuable** than any riches (Proverbs 8, Job 20)

6. Wisdom is **evident**- it can be proven and observed by behavior that demonstrates righteousness, justice and compassion (Proverbs 1:3, Psalms 15 and 26)

7. Wisdom is **available** to young and old alike (Proverbs 1:4, Job 32)

8. And finally, wisdom is a **gift from God** that can be received simply by asking for it (Job 38:36, 2 Chronicles 1:10-11, James 1:5)

The passages cited are but a few of the dozens of examples found in scripture that further underscore each of the eight characteristics of wisdom I have highlighted. We should always be asking ourselves if we are continually learning and teaching God's wisdom, valuing it and allowing it to increase in our lives as demonstrated in our behaviors.

There is one more characteristic of wisdom worth reflecting upon today. Read Ecclesiastes 1:18 (NASB):

Because in much wisdom there is much grief, and increasing knowledge results in increasing pain.

In much wisdom there is much grief? At first blush, this seems incongruous with all of the other passages about wisdom. And yet, upon deeper reflection, I have found this to be very true in life. The more of God's wisdom I absorb, the greater my awareness of the pain around me. The traumas of abused children, pain associated with addiction, injustice, and poverty, the grief of broken hearts and wounded souls, the immediate and lifelong consequences of sin on people, communities and all of creation—these all become more profoundly seen, felt and understood.

It is only when we can truly see, hear and feel the pain and grief of others through the eyes and with the wisdom of God that we can be also used by Him to be His hands and feet, bringing the healing touch of His compassion, grace and restoration to the world. May we all yearn for this kind of wisdom and also for the grace and courage to act upon what we learn!

Today's hymn for meditation and reflection is "Cuando el Pobre"

Spanish version:
https://www.youtube.com/watch?v=5dbWJBHZ428
English version:
https://www.youtube.com/watch?v=8AJvB4DwjNQ

But if any of you lacks wisdom, let him ask of God, who gives to all generously and without reproach, and it will be given to him.(James 1:5)

Day 26 – Hidden Parts

Read Verse 6

Behold, You desire truth in the innermost being, And in the hidden part You will make me know wisdom.

This is the third and final day of reflecting on verse six. We have looked at the meanings of "truth" and "wisdom" and today we will focus on our "innermost being" and "hidden part."

What exactly is our innermost being and our hidden part? Is it that deep part of our hearts only the dearest few get to see? Is it our spirit? Our soul? However we define it, I believe this innermost, hidden part of ourselves is often buried under layer upon layer of protective and decorative coverings until we have forgotten that it is even there.

This reminds me of a conversation I had with my husband about the work he has been doing refinishing some woodwork in our 100-year-old home. We captured this conversation in our book, ***"Are We There Yet? The Ultimate Road Trip Adopting and Raising 22 Kids"*** (2013, Carpenter's Son Publishing) and I'd like to share an excerpt here:

"Working on this wood gives me a lot of time to think," Hector *says on a Friday evening when I come home. "I started out wondering why anyone would put layers and layers of paint on this beautiful woodwork. The paint is so much uglier than the natural beauty of the wood underneath."*

"I know. I just don't get it, but I guess it was the fashion at the time," I say.

"Right, exactly. Someone did it because they thought they were improving upon the original, making it more beautiful than it was before. And layers got added on top of layers, so it becomes a slow and tedious process to remove it all."

"I'm glad you're stripping it; it'll be so much nicer when you finish. Just look at this section that you've done. It's so lovely," I say, running my hand along the panel.

"I'm happy about it too, but I want to share with you the spiritual truth I'm gleaning as I work."

"OK."

"You see, in our own lives, we're often like the people who added layers of paint, covering up the natural wood. How often do we pile stuff onto ourselves, or our kids, thinking we are making improvements, when all we are doing is hiding the natural beauty within? Then, when we finally realize that all this added junk has to come off, it's such a tedious process, removing all the gunk, so the natural beauty has a chance to shine through again. Sometimes I think God is working on me little by little, slowly scraping off the layers of stuff I plastered all over myself, thinking I was making improvements. Through all my life experiences, God is showing me that it's what's underneath all the stuff that matters. He has to keep working on me because I've added a heck of a lot of layers over the years."

"You know, that makes a lot of sense. I'm sure the people who painted this wood thought they were doing a good thing and didn't realize people like us would later come along and say, 'What were they thinking?' Just like we sometimes do really stupid stuff thinking it makes total sense, while others are shaking their heads and saying, 'What were they thinking?'"

"Exactly. And even when it looks like I'm done, there is still more gunk in the little grooves. It takes special tools to really get deep down in those grooves and get the gunk out. It would be easy to say it's not worth it or it doesn't matter—but come here, let me show you something."

He walks me over to another part of the room.

"Look at this panel. This one is completely finished—even the tiniest grooves. Now what do you think?"

"Spectacular. And yes, what a difference. It really was worth all your effort to get every last bit of gunk out. You've really given me something to think about."

"I try to do that once in a while," he laughs."

This Psalm reminds us not to settle for superficial wisdom, or for lacquered facades that mask as truth. We may have distorted images of who God is or what constitutes truth based upon our own human experiences and relationships, over-simplified Sunday lessons, erroneous but fiercely held cultural interpretations, customs or conventions, personal or social biases, prejudices and institutional racism or other forms of injustice. Each of these adds its own distinct layer of paint to the underlying natural beauty, and although we, or someone, thought it was right, beautiful, wise and truth-filled at the time, we fail to realize the extent to which we have buried that which is genuinely true and wise under all of these layers.

Just as Hector learned while working on the woodwork, getting down to the hidden part can be a slow, laborious process and may require special tools and oceans of patience. But the end result is nothing short of spectacular.

Will you pray with me today, *"Lord, help me to examine my heart and my inner being. Give me the patience and perseverance to allow your truth and wisdom to penetrate all the way down into my hidden places. Give me the courage to take risks and ask questions, never settling for a false veneer of truth, but always digging deeper, to expose my hidden parts to Your wisdom and your truth. Amen."*

Listen to "You are my Hiding Place" while writing a few notes in your journal today about the layers of veneer that need to be stripped away to get to the hidden part of your own heart.

https://www.youtube.com/watch?v=RzqpkMJxyss

Day 27 – Broken

Read Verses 16-17

16 For You do not delight in sacrifice, otherwise I would give it; You are not pleased with burnt offering. 17 The sacrifices of God are a broken spirit; A broken and a contrite heart, O God, You will not despise.

Verses 16-17 fit into two of our theme-areas, so we will look at them today and again next week when our topic is "Joy." For today, let's focus on the word "broken" as it appears twice here. A condition of developing and maintaining truth and wisdom in our inner being is to recognize, acknowledge and bring before God our own broken hearts and spirits as our worshipful sacrifice.

As I contemplated the connection between "truth in the inner being" and broken hearts and spirits, an image of a string of Christmas tree lights popped into my head. Some sets of lights are designed so that if one bulb burns out, the rest remain lit, yet the burnt-out bulb diminishes the overall effect of the string. In some ways, this bulb represents the "brokenness" of an otherwise "living" Christian. Plugged in at the source, this Christian is mostly connected to and in tune with the Holy Spirit, producing light (or fruit), honoring God and leading others to Him by the glow of her light. As she gains truth and wisdom in her inner being, she recognizes the "burnt out" bulbs in her life, offering them up to God and allowing Him to guide her as she take steps to replace them with working "bulbs."

Imagine replacing a bulb on a string of lights already wrapped around the tree. It's difficult to do, often requiring a stepladder and an assistant. It involves acquiring a good bulb, climbing the ladder, untwisting the bad bulb (which may be "stuck") and then replacing it. So too, sometimes the changes we need to make in our lives to root out the "broken bulbs" and replace them with His truth and wisdom will take work, multiple steps, help from others and extra effort to deal with things that are "stuck".

There are also strings of lights designed in such a way that if one bulb is bad, the whole string of lights goes dark, even when connected to a good power source. How easy it is to view the whole string as bad and throw it away. Is it really worth the effort to find and replace the bad bulb? Often the bad bulb is not apparent to the naked eye—it may look good on the outside, but still not be producing light. So it is only by the tedious process of testing each bulb one-by-one that we eventually discover the bad one. We also cannot tell by looking at the whole string if there is only one bad bulb or two, three or more. If only there was an easy way to immediately spot the bad bulbs and quickly replace them!

How thankful I am that God doesn't decide to cast us aside and throw us out when we have a "bad bulb" (or two or twenty) in our life because we aren't worth the time and effort needed to locate and change the bad bulbs. As we seek truth and wisdom in our inner being, God gives us the discernment needed to find the dead bulb(s) and replace them.

It's critical to seek God's discernment for this task. It does no good to randomly pick a bulb to replace—that will not "fix" the string of lights. Nor will using some criteria such as "replace all green bulbs." In other words, change, just for the sake of change, does not produce the desired outcome. It produces only more dead bulbs and inner brokenness.

But when we present our broken hearts and spirits to the living God, He takes that brokenness, replacing it with His life-giving truth and wisdom in our deep and hidden places. The outcome is a glittering string of lights that is shining brightly from beginning to end—giving honor and glory to God.

Will you join me today in presenting all of our broken bulbs to the living God?

As you meditate on today's reflection, making notes in your journal, listen to "Beauty for Brokenness" **https://www.youtube.com/watch?v=SxfBh9ay8gE**

And "In Brokenness I Come to You" **https://www.youtube.com/watch?v=opBeDVq2CSA**

Day 28 – Revived

Read Verses 16-17

16 For You do not delight in sacrifice, otherwise I would give it; You are not pleased with burnt offering. 17 The sacrifices of God are a broken spirit; A broken and a contrite heart, O God, You will not despise.

Today is the last day of the theme "Truth in the Inner Being." We have learned that God wants us to speak truth even to ourselves, difficult as that is at times. In so doing we can become more holy, more closely aligned with the true character of God. We've learned that wisdom is a precious gift from God, available to us merely for the asking, but brings with it new glimpses of the consequences of sin in the word and the pain and grief many of our fellow sojourners suffer. Wisdom calls upon us to act as God's hands and feet bringing His grace into a hurting world. God has shown us that our own inner being is often hidden deeply under layers and layers of false veneers, but that He will give us the tools to scrape off those layers and reveal the incredible beauty that lies beneath. Finally we have seen that even when we are broken in these deep, hidden places, God does not cast us aside, but instead gives us the courage and the discernment to replace the "broken bulbs" so that we can shine for Him again.

And so, as we spend one last day on this topic, we read these words, *"a contrite heart, O God, You will not despise."*

Picking up where we left off yesterday, enjoying the revelation that God does not toss us aside when we have one or more "burnt bulbs" on our string of lights, we find that this also has something to teach us about our own self-esteem and our relationships with others.

How often do I become so discouraged and down on myself that I feel useless, worthless, hopeless? I feel that if I am not producing certain fruits (if I have a few dead bulbs) that I am no good as a parent, a professional or even as a human being. And how easy it is, too, to look at another person that is struggling with a particular challenge or sin and simply become discouraged, frustrated, disgusted or hopeless; wanting to simply give up on that person rather than believe that, with God's help, that person too can be changed and transformed from a seemingly useless string of non-working lights to a glowing, light-producing valued and worthy citizen in the kingdom of God. I wonder how often I might be the one with the good bulb in my pocket that one of my children, grandchildren or neighbors needs, and yet I don't make the effort to help them change the bad bulbs in their life because I am "burnt out" myself?

There is good news! It is precisely in these moments of disgust or despair, of disappointment or defeat that our hearts are not merely cracked, but broken wide open—contrite. These are the moments when God comes to us with a promise. What does he have to say to the one who comes to Him with a *contrite heart?*

Read Isaiah 57:15 (NASB):

For thus says the high and exalted One Who lives forever, whose name is Holy, "I dwell on a high and holy place, And also with the contrite and lowly of spirit In order to revive the spirit of the lowly And to revive the heart of the contrite.

"To revive the heart of the contrite."

The God of the universe, the God who came down to our broken earth and lived as one among his broken people, the God who has adopted us as his very own children and calls us by name—*This God* desires to revive our hearts.

Can there be any nugget of wisdom more wonderful than this?

Be refreshed! Be revived! Shine on!

As we end this week, write a few notes in your journal and make this song your prayer: "Revive Us Again"

https://www.youtube.com/watch?v=46jkJqbSPYg

Day 29 – Passion

Read Psalm 51

Yesterday's topic, "Revive!" was the perfect way to make the transition to the topic of "Joy!" which will be our theme all of this week. As we have delved deeper and deeper into this Psalm, we have engaged our minds, exploring nuances and unearthed meanings behind key words, phrases and concepts. We have also asked God to open our Spirit to His Spirit and prayed to become more and more like Him each day.

As we transition now to week five, it is time again to reflect upon the entire Psalm and I'd like to invite you to focus on engaging your heart. Today take a few moments to listen to the complete Psalm read or sung aloud.

You can ask a friend to read it to you, read it aloud yourself, recording it and then playing it back. You may have your own audio version of the Bible. Below are links to a couple of other options. Whichever option you choose, close your eyes as you listen and allow the words to penetrate your heart and allow yourself to fully experience the feelings elicited by this Psalm.

Psalms 51, Sons of Korah:
https://www.youtube.com/watch?v=pbILLkOmLdc
Psalms 51: Ramzi Adcock:
https://www.youtube.com/watch?v=_iC7O3zcqF8
Psalms 51: King James Bible:
https://www.youtube.com/watch?v=pr2ogEgxT4A

Be gracious to me, O God, according to Your lovingkindness; According to the greatness of Your compassion blot out my transgressions. ²Wash me thoroughly from my iniquity And cleanse me from my sin.

71

3 For I know my transgressions, And my sin is ever before me. 4 Against You, You only, I have sinned And done what is evil in Your sight, So that You are justified when You speak And blameless when You judge.

5 Behold, I was brought forth in iniquity, And in sin my mother conceived me. 6 Behold, You desire truth in the innermost being, And in the hidden part You will make me know wisdom. 7 Purify me with hyssop, and I shall be clean; Wash me, and I shall be whiter than snow. 8 Make me to hear joy and gladness, Let the bones which You have broken rejoice. 9 Hide Your face from my sins And blot out all my iniquities.

10 Create in me a clean heart, O God, And renew a steadfast spirit within me. 11 Do not cast me away from Your presence And do not take Your Holy Spirit from me. 12 Restore to me the joy of Your salvation And sustain me with a willing spirit. 13 Then I will teach transgressors Your ways, And sinners will be converted to You.

14 Deliver me from bloodguiltiness, O God, the God of my salvation; Then my tongue will joyfully sing of Your righteousness. 15 O Lord, open my lips, That my mouth may declare Your praise. 16 For You do not delight in sacrifice, otherwise I would give it; You are not pleased with burnt offering. 17 The sacrifices of God are a broken spirit; A broken and a contrite heart, O God, You will not despise.

18 By Your favor do good to Zion; [n]Build the walls of Jerusalem. 19 Then You will delight in[J]righteous sacrifices, In burnt offering and whole burnt offering; Then young bulls will be offered on Your altar.

Sit quietly with your emotions for a few moments. Write a few reflections in your journal. Allow God to touch your heart and awaken your feelings.

Do you feel it? Passion? This Psalm is overflowing with passion. No matter who reads it or in which version or translation, it stirs up many emotions from grief and sorrow to unspeakable joy, from longing to wonder and gratitude.

God is the creator of emotions. He gave us the ability to experience love, joy, pain, sorrow and the entire panoply of feelings that course through our beings each and every day. He longs for us to engage our whole heart with all of our emotions and passions as we pursue His heart.

*"I know all the things you do, that you are neither hot nor cold. I wish that you were one or the other! **16** But since you are like lukewarm water, neither hot nor cold, I will spit you out of my mouth! (Revelation 3:15-16, NLT)*

One of the great challenges when working with children who have experienced trauma is the challenge of helping them to recognize, feel and express a full range of emotions. As a result of the pain they have suffered, they are at once numb to many emotions and at the same time hyper-sensitive to negative emotions—always on guard for even the slightest hint that someone around them may be ready to explode in anger, placing them in great danger. Little-by-little it is the job of the caring adults in their lives to re-awaken their hearts and help them discover that it is both safe and valuable to feel, to feel deeply, and to express their own emotions. This is critical to the healing process.

So today I pray that we, too, will give our whole hearts to God and ask him to give us the courage to come to him with all of our emotions. To be passionate in our embrace. To be stirred out of a lukewarm stasis into the hot and cold world of an on-fire faith.

Let's end our time today listening to a musical composition that stirs the emotions. Select a piece that really ignites your passions. Whether that means Bach or rap, jazz or blues, close your eyes and lose yourself in the music. Experience it. Feel it. Ignite your passions!

Here are two very different but worthy examples: (Bach and jazz)

https://www.youtube.com/watch?v=UM5BqVpoRcA
https://www.youtube.com/watch?v=j1bWqViY5F4

Day 30 – Introduction to Theme 5

"Joy!"

Read Verses 8, 12, 16-17

⁸ Make me to hear joy and gladness, Let the bones which You have broken rejoice.

¹² Restore to me the joy of Your salvation And sustain me with a willing spirit.

¹⁶ For You do not delight in sacrifice, otherwise I would give it; You are not pleased with burnt offering. ¹⁷ The sacrifices of God are a broken spirit; A broken and a contrite heart, O God, You will not despise.

"I've got the joy, joy, joy, joy down in my heart!" As the icy grip of winter is finally loosening just a bit here in Philadelphia, I am so looking forward to the warmth of spring and an entire week to focus on the theme of "Joy!"

Psalm 51 speaks of joy three times. The first time, David says, *"Make me to hear joy and gladness."* In the second instance David cries out *"Restore to me the joy of Your salvation."* And finally we read of the joy (delight) that God himself experiences from us when we offer true worship to Him.

Hearing, holding onto and giving back joy. We'll consider it from each of these perspectives throughout the week. But first, let's just make a joyful noise together.

We collect Christmas tree ornaments. This collection began the first year we were married when one of our dearest friends gave us a small simple ornament. This hand-made, now fading cross-stitch hanging from a bit of red ribbon says, "JOY." We have learned about and experienced joy in many ways over the years, but several of the most valuable lessons about joy we learned from Pam, the friend who made this ornament.

In her quiet way, she shared her life with us and through her we learned of the joy that can be found in simple, everyday pleasures. The joy of a good home-cooked pot of potato-corn soup. The joy of sitting outside on a warm summer evening, with friends, playing softball, watching the children play. The joy of scraping and painting a room. The joy of a good marriage. The joy of learning a new song, *"Jubilate Deo"* and then using it to worship our God together.

There is more than one word in each of the original biblical languages that is translated as "joy." Depending upon which translation you read, you will find anywhere between 200-300 verses containing the word "joy" and many more when you add words such as "joyful," and "rejoice."

We find joy referenced when babies are born, marriages are celebrated, new believers enter the kingdom, and when sinners repent. We see joy expressed through clapping, singing, dancing and feasting. Joy is evident in the majesty of creation, and the very creation itself expresses joy. While dozens of the references to joy are found, naturally, in the Psalms, it is interesting to note that even in one of the most challenging books of the Bible—Job—joy is referenced many times.

And it is for this reason, that joy can be found even in the story of Job, that our little "Joy" ornament hangs front and center every year on our tree. "Joy" is not only the theme of the tree but of our family. This simple, faded ornament says that in spite of all the hard times, the challenges, the sorrows "JOY", indeed, stands front and center in our lives in all of its brazen nosiness and messiness. Jubilate Deo indeed!

Make a joyful noise unto the Lord, all ye lands. Serve the Lord with gladness: come before his presence with singing. (Psalm 100 1-2, KJV)

Today, take out your journal, open to a fresh page and make a list of all the things that bring you joy. Little things and big things. Every day things and once-in-a-blue-moon things. Come back to this page and add to it throughout the week.

When you are finished and your hand is exhausted from all the writing, make some noise. Make a joyful noise. Sing. Dance. Clap your hands. Don't be shy and don't be quiet. Let the sound of joy fill your heart and your home.

Make a joyful noise to the Lord! Sing it loud and sing it strong. Rejoice!

There are many hymns and songs of joy you can listen and sing-along to today. Find your own favorite – here is one to get your started – I dare you to listen to this without jumping up and joining in!

https://www.youtube.com/watch?v=VQ86ZP6kxSc

Day 31 – Make Me!

Read Verse 8

8 Make me to hear joy and gladness, Let the bones which You have broken rejoice.

"You can't make me, nah-nah-nah-nah-nah!"

"Go ahead, I dare you, make me!"

Childhood taunts we have all heard and perhaps spoken in our own youth. Sometimes spoken out of anger, other times prompted by hurt feelings, and still other times by haughty indignation. "Make me!" we cry, fully believing we have just issued the impossible challenge. We will not cave-in, we will not cry uncle, we will not, we will not.

I am pretty sure no Bible scholar has suggested that David was taunting God when he cried out, *"Make me to hear joy and gladness"* and yet, given my experiences with wounded children, I cannot read these words any other way.

Children who came into our home with deep wounds and a multitude of scars from their experiences with trauma, abuse, neglect or abandonment often appeared to have a chip on their shoulder, a chip that said, *"I dare you! Make me trust again. Make me hope again. You won't succeed; no one has."*

One particular teenage daughter simply never smiled. One day, exasperated as I tried to get just one picture of her with a smile on her face, I asked her, *"Why can't you just give me one smile?"*

I have never forgotten her reply, *"You want a fake smile, I'll give it to you. But don't get the idea that you can make me feel like smiling. You can't make me happy. You can't make me want to smile. I am dead inside and nothing you do is going to change that."*

Have you ever felt that way? Dead inside?

The world we live in is a brutal place. Many have experienced the pain of physical or sexual assaults. Domestic abuse in the home or random violence in the community. Many bear scars from the death or betrayal of a loved one while the ravages of emotional abuse or bullying erode the confidence and self-esteem of others. Some wounds are self-inflicted as we batter our own minds, bodies and spirits with alcohol, drugs, over-eating, unhealthy sexual liaisons, pornography or an unending quest for money and status. Then there are those who are simply worn down, physically, emotionally and spiritually numbed by what they lack—lack of food, lack of a home, lack of love or even a moment of human kindness.

Bones, hearts, minds and spirits are broken, crushed, pulverized. How can anyone who has experienced such brokenness ever know joy and gladness again?

Our daughter did smile for the picture on the day when we had that unforgettable conversation. An overly bright fake smile. It was heartbreaking. That photograph which captured her hollow, empty smile haunted me for a long time.

Eventually, she smiled for real and I was easily able to see the difference. In the real smile, her eyes glowed with hope, the corners of her mouth tickled by joy. The uncompromising, unconditional, unwavering love of both God and family pierced the wall she had built around her heart. It didn't happen overnight. It took time, patience and an abiding faith that love would indeed prevail. When that day came, the day of the real smile, we knew that *the bones that had been broken rejoiced.*

Don't be afraid to *dare* God to make you smile, make you laugh, make you to know joy and gladness. He can and He will. He will make you to know joy. He will uphold you. The bones that are broken will indeed rejoice. Hallelujah!

Today, reflect upon what it means when God makes you feel joy. Write in your journal and listen to the Winans sing, "Uphold Me"

https://www.youtube.com/watch?v=glontj6o6HA

Day 32 – Hearing

Read Verse 8

8 Make me to hear joy and gladness, Let the bones which You have broken rejoice.

Yesterday, we examined this verse from the perspective of one whose bones, heart and spirit are broken. Can God really "make" a person—even me—experience joy and gladness when he or she—or I—feel dead inside? We learned that God can, indeed, work slowly and patiently bringing those dead bones to life and bringing joy and gladness back to even the hardest heart.

Today, we turn to the concept of hearing joy and gladness. *Make me to hear joy and gladness,"* our psalmist says. On Day 23 of our journey, we reflected on the concepts of being present and tuning-in. We likened tuning-in to God to the process of tuning-in to a radio station. Even when God's program is "on the air" we will not hear it if our radio is not on, volume turned up and the dial "tuned-in" to the correct station. If those conditions are not met, we will find ourselves listening only to static, or to the worldly noise offered by other stations.

As we get better at tuning-in to God through prayer, confession of sin, meditation, cleansing, receiving the new heart He gives us and walking in the light of His truth and wisdom, this verse tells us that we can expect to hear joy and gladness. Tuning-in to God is meant to result in a joy-filled life. His "channel" on our radio is not going to be filled with doom and gloom. Joy will abound!

Yet, sometimes we are so focused on the grief and sorrows both within us and around us that we forget to listen for the joy that He offers. How do we hear the joy?

We have to listen for it.

Leaders in fields ranging from social work to education to sales and marketing to business management understand that active listening requires more than merely hearing. Research highlights that most people retain as little as 25% of what they hear, so agency and company leaders often bring in experts to train their staff in the art and skill of active and appreciative listening. Active listening involves using more than just our ears—it employs all five of our senses as well as our heart and spirit.

When Jesus began teaching in parables (read Matthew chapter 13) He gave his disciples a lesson on the difference between merely hearing, and hearing with understanding (listening).

But blessed are your eyes, because they see; and your ears, because they hear,

Jesus tells them in verse 16. In Romans 10:17, we learn that this deeper hearing comes from one place: *faith comes from hearing, and hearing by the word of Christ.*

Throughout scripture the renewed and revived faith that comes from hearing the word has an immediate impact: joy overflows. When new believers hear the word, they respond with joy. When those who had strayed return to the word, the rejoicing is so loud it can be heard from afar:

"And on that day they offered great sacrifices and rejoiced because God had given them great joy, even the women and children rejoiced, so that the joy of Jerusalem was heard from afar." (Nehemiah 12:43 NASB)

We hear joy when we listen for it. And we listen for it when we believe.

Remember that list of things that bring you joy I asked you to write at the beginning of this week? Pull it out again now. Look at it and ask yourself, "Where do I *hear* joy? When do I *listen* for joy?

Do I wake up in the morning expecting to experience joy and gladness throughout the day? Do I use all of my senses to listen for and hear the joy that abounds around me? Do I tune-in to joy throughout the day? Do I lay my weary bones down at the end of the day grateful for the joy I heard and the gladness that filled my heart on this day?

Try this experiment. Close your eyes and imagine yourself in your favorite spot in your own home. Now breathe slowly and engage all five of your senses as you immerse yourself into being present in that spot.

Breathe slowly – in, out, in, out. What do you see when you look around? Are you inside or outside? Do you see photographs, people, nature, furnishings, colors? What do you see? Do you see joy?

Breathe slowly – in, out, in, out. What do you hear in this spot? Food cooking and sizzling? Nature? Music? Children playing? Traffic? Conversations? What do you hear? Do you hear joy?

Breathe slowly – in, out, in, out. What do you smell and taste? Favorite foods? Familiar odors – someone's perfume? Nature or animal odors? What do you taste? Food? Beverage? Gum? Imagine the smells and tastes. Do you taste and smell joy?

Breathe slowly – in, out, in, out. What are the textures you are touching? The wind or breeze on your face? The nubby fabric of a sofa? Soft clothing against your skin? The hard floor under your feet? What are the textures surrounding you? Can you touch joy?

Breathe slowly – in, out, in, out. Now notice how you feel – emotionally – in this place. How does your body feel? How about your spirit? Can you experience joy here in this everyday place?

Hearing joy and experiencing gladness is not meant to be reserved for special occasions. Following God is not meant to be a tedious trek, rigidly adhering to a religious straitjacket of do's and don'ts. We were created to hear and experience joy every day, everywhere. Even in the messiness of life, as we journey towards healing, wholeness and the fullness of redemption. Joy is not for later; it is for the here and the now.

Are you ready to hear joy in a new way today?

"The Lord has done great things for us, we are filled with joy!" Listen to Psalm 126, set to music:
https://www.youtube.com/watch?v=sIFXqcFGHjA
and experience joy.

Day 33 – Aha!

Read Verse 12

12 Restore to me the joy of Your salvation And sustain me with a willing spirit.

Today we turn to the second time in this Psalm David seeks joy, crying out *"Restore to me the joy of your salvation."* The joy of salvation, the joy of untainted fellowship with the creator of the entire universe.

There are many things that can be said about the meaning of salvation, the word and its variations appear dozens of times throughout scripture. Volumes of books, expositions and sermons have been written on this topic. But for our experience of salvation to be characterized by joy it must be more than just head-knowledge. The reality of salvation must flood our hearts and spirits.

We need a salvation "aha!" moment. There are two qualities of salvation that have given me "aha" moments over the years. The first was when the reality of being rescued when all hope seemed lost finally sunk in. The second was when I was realized that with salvation, God had given me a whole new lens for seeing the world around me. Perhaps you have had similar "aha" moments in your own faith journey.

The word salvation is synonymous with the word "rescue." To appreciate the value of being rescued, we have to have at least a glimpse of what we are being rescued from. For me, this happened in a ditch on the side of the road. I had been driving all-night with one of my daughters and her infant son and began getting sleepy around three in the morning.

The next thing I knew, I was in a ditch, upside down, pinned between the steering wheel and door. My grandson was crying and my daughter was unconscious. I was terrified that we'd never get out. Who would see us at this hour? From time to time, I'd see the glimmer of headlights on the road above. No one stopped.

Finally, a trucker stopped. I could hardly express my gratitude. He stayed with us until an ambulance came. My daughter was fine, and my grandson had a mild concussion. I had several broken bones including my right wrist. This required surgery and the insertion of metal pins so that I could be "fixed."

Whenever I think of my heroic trucker, I re-live my "aha" moment about my salvation in Christ. In that ditch on the side of the road I experienced genuine terror that I would never be rescued and that the three of us would die right there. I have also experienced moments of emotional and spiritual terror, moments when everything about my life feels hopeless and death seems inevitable.

The joy that flooded my entire being when that trucker stopped and raised us out of that ditch is but a hint of the overwhelming joy of salvation when we accept, understand and appreciate the fact that we are already raised out of every ditch and dark valley we may temporarily fall into along life's journey. We have already been rescued before we even realize we are in the ditch! It is done, finished, we are completely restored to light, life and wholeness. Aha!

Beyond rescuing us, when God saves us He also gives us new eyes for seeing the world.

What touched me so deeply about the trucker, and resulted in my second "aha" moment was that he stopped and stayed with us—not knowing if we could be saved, or "fixed." It cost him time, took him out of his way, and set him back on his route.

I think of him often when I get discouraged that I can't always "fix" everything for my children, or when I don't see complete healing from the damage and injuries they sustained early in their lives—whether it's the physical injuries such as Dylan's who was a shaken baby, or some of the deeper emotionally "damages" so many of our kids sustained by all kinds of brutal early life experiences. I'm reminded to look beyond the "wreck" to see hope and possibilities for healing, just as the trucker did for us.

"Aha!" It is not up to me to decide whom God will save, but rather to be willing to stop and come alongside every person He brings into my life in love. If I know the true joy of salvation, it will always be worth my time to reach out to someone in a ditch, regardless of what the outcome may be. The outcome is in God's hands, God's mercy, however, can be offered through my hands. My feet. My heart, shared freely because of the joy of my salvation.

"Aha!"

Will you pray with me today, *"God grant us Your eyes so that we might never miss an "aha" moment you have provided for us, and in sharing these moments, may we ever more deeply know the joy of our salvation. Amen."*

"Open My Eyes That I May See" is the perfect accompaniment for today as you write a few notes in your journal recalling "aha!" moments in your own life. **https://www.youtube.com/watch?v=M7M5lcxDD3Y**

Day 34 – Sustain Me

Read Verse 12

12 Restore to me the joy of Your salvation And sustain me with a willing spirit.

Sustain. Uphold. Strengthen. Preserve. Keep from falling.

"Sustain me with a willing spirit." Hold me up, Lord. Keep me from falling. David realizes here that in spite of having journeyed to the pit and explored the evil of his own sin; in spite of traveling to the mountain top and reveling in the unfailing, enduring holiness, love and compassion of his God; in spite of being bathed and scrubbed and thoroughly cleansed; in spite of receiving a new heart—in spite of all of these things, he is still in danger of falling.

He doesn't want to fall. Again.

So he beseeches God, *"Sustain me."* Hold me up.

He has utter confidence that God will follow through. He rests in the peace and assurance that the God of the universe will not let him fall. Why does he have this confidence? The answer is found in the second clause, *"with a willing spirit."*

"Willing spirit" is also translated as a "free" spirit and a "spirit of liberty." The most common cross-reference seized by commentators is Romans 8:15-16 (NASB):

15 For you have not received a spirit of slavery leading to fear again, but you have received a spirit of adoption as sons by which we cry out, "Abba! Father!" 16 The Spirit Himself testifies with our spirit that we are children of God,

The "free" and "willing" spirit of Psalm 51 is contrasted with the spirit of fear and slavery found in Romans 8. We not only find the **joy** of our salvation, but it can be **sustained** when we embrace the freedom we have in Christ. Our walk of faith is not meant to be characterized by a "lions and tigers and bears, Oh my!" attitude of fear, but by the spirit of freedom that comes from knowing we are the adopted children of the living God.

I've always loved this passage because of its reference to adoption. When children who cannot remain with their families of origin enter foster care, they are awash in a sea of fear. One of our oldest sons, adopted as a teen, phrased it this way:

"This is how it is in foster care, you always have to move from foster home to foster home and you don't have any say in this. You always have to adapt to new people and new kids and new schools. Sometimes you feel like you are going crazy inside. You feel left out, tossed like dirt, trash. This is a big deal that people don't realize.

No level of earthly success can erase the underlying fear that persists in the heart of a child who never knew the unconditional love of a family that would be his forever. One young man who grew up in foster care was so resilient that he put himself through college, obtained a master's degree and achieved a high level of success in his career. Yet, he told me, *"There is not a day that goes by that I don't fear that the bottom will fall out."* This young man had never received the gift of adoption, his entire childhood had been lived out in foster care and the legacy of fear followed him like a rabid dog even into his successful adult years.

It is only when children who can't return to their birth parents finally experience the security of adoption that they can let go of fear and begin to heal from trauma. To continue in my son's words:

And then I moved one last time, to my adoptive family and I realized that I had choices and hope for a future. All kids deserve families. They need a family, to have someone, this is father, this is mother. "Love, always, forever and no matter what" that is what adoption means to me, and that is what all kids deserve.

It is profound that God chose the word "adoption" to underscore our relationship within the circle of his family. It is this spirit, the spirit of adoption as sons and daughters, which will sustain us.

Will you pray with me today, *"Abba, father, thank you for adopting me as your child, making me a member of your family always, forever and no matter what. Help me to rest in the confidence that this is the spirit that will sustain me today and always. Amen."*

Here is a precious song to enjoy while writing today's reflections in your journal: "Though I was born an Orphan" **https://www.youtube.com/watch?v=WRRSFxiiDpA**

Day 35 – Delight

Read Verses 16-17

16 For You do not delight in sacrifice, otherwise I would give it; You are not pleased with burnt offering. 17 The sacrifices of God are a broken spirit; A broken and a contrite heart, O God, You will not despise.

Verses sixteen and seventeen are a couplet that cannot be easily separated; yet they also related to two of our themes for these reflections. So we focused on the broken spirit and contrite heart of verse seventeen last week while covering the theme of "Truth in the Inner Being." Today, we highlight the words "delight" and "pleased" in verse sixteen as they relate to this week's theme of "Joy."

This is the third place where our psalmist talks about joy. This time it is in terms of God himself experiencing joy from us, taking delight in our true worship, not the "burnt offering" type of sacrifice, but a "broken and contrite heart". Imagine that, God not only gives us a new heart and a new life overflowing with abundant joy, but He also receives joy from us!

I understand this best when I remember that God is not just our "Father" (with a capital "F") but also our "daddy," our "Abba," our "pappa." And in that role, he takes delight in us much as we take delight in our own children and grandchildren. A messy hand-crayoned card from a 5-year old or a spontaneous hug from a pre-teen is guaranteed to provide pure pleasure!

I have a son who rejected us as his parents for several years. He refused to call us "mom" and "dad," rejecting our core values. During these years he occasionally gave us gifts on special occasions. Those gifts only further intensified my grief over our broken relationship; they did not bring me joy.

Now, he's returned to the family fold. He doesn't make a lot of money, but he does things to demonstrate his love for and commitment to the family like babysitting for his nieces and nephews. When I see him wrestling my 5-year-old grandson and hear them both laughing the delight I feel is deep and genuine.

God does not delight in routine or legalistic sacrifices. He desires the broken and contrite heart we discussed last week, but He also describes what he desires in two of the most-cited cross-references to this particular verse. Two of my favorite scriptures! Notice the word *"delight"* in each of these verses, and pay attention to what we can do that will truly bring delight to our "Abba."

Hosea 6 (read the whole chapter. I have cited part of verses 3 and 6)

"3: So let us know, let us press on to know the Lord . . . . 6: For I delight in loyalty rather than sacrifice, And in the knowledge of God rather than burnt offerings.

Micah 6: 6-8

6:With what shall I come to the Lord And bow myself before the God on high? Shall I come to Him with burnt offerings, With yearling calves?

7 Does the Lord take delight in thousands of rams, In ten thousand rivers of oil? Shall I present my firstborn for my rebellious acts, The fruit of my body for the sin of my soul? He has showed you, O man, what is good. And what does the Lord require of you? To act justly, and to love mercy. And to walk humbly with your God.

What can I do to bring delight to my "daddy?"

Press on to know Him—meditate on His word day and night.

Act justly – treat others with fairness and dignity, be the voice calling out for justice in an increasingly unjust world.

Love mercy – remember, God has spared *us* from the consequences we deserve—*love mercy, share mercy, restore mercy to our broken world.*

And knowing that God, in his amazing Grace has given us so much goodness that we do not deserve – **walk humbly, and joyfully and hopefully with our God**.

Will you pray this prayer with me: *"Abba, Father, May each of us bring delight to you today as we walk with you in childlike joy. Amen."*

How do you delight your daddy? Jot a few reflections in your journal, while listening to Micah 6:8 set to music:

https://www.youtube.com/watch?v=NWlHndKJ6rI
https://www.youtube.com/watch?v=xN38zJKrPJc

Day 36 – Personal

Read Psalm 51

As we enter our final week of this study, we begin by reading the Psalm in its entirety once again. As you read it today, notice how many times the words, "I," "me," and "my" are repeated. This psalm is absolutely both universal and timeless in its truths, but at its core it is deeply personal.

Today, make it personal. In the quiet of your heart make this between you and God alone.

Be gracious to me, O God, according to Your lovingkindness; According to the greatness of Your compassion blot out my transgressions. ²Wash me thoroughly from my iniquity And cleanse me from my sin. ³For I know my transgressions, And my sin is ever before me. ⁴Against You, You only, I have sinned And done what is evil in Your sight, So that You are justified when You speak And blameless when You judge.

⁵Behold, I was brought forth in iniquity, And in sin my mother conceived me. ⁶Behold, You desire truth in the innermost being, And in the hidden part You will make me know wisdom. ⁷Purify me with hyssop, and I shall be clean; Wash me, and I shall be whiter than snow. ⁸Make me to hear joy and gladness, Let the bones which You have broken rejoice. ⁹Hide Your face from my sins And blot out all my iniquities.

¹⁰Create in me a clean heart, O God, And renew a steadfast spirit within me. ¹¹Do not cast me away from Your presence And do not take Your Holy Spirit from me. ¹²Restore to me the joy of Your salvation And sustain me with a willing spirit. *13 Then I will teach transgressors Your ways, And sinners will be converted to You.*

14 Deliver me from bloodguiltiness, O God, the God of my salvation; Then my tongue will joyfully sing of Your righteousness. 15 O Lord, open my lips, That my mouth may declare Your praise. 16 For You do not delight in sacrifice, otherwise I would give it; You are not pleased with burnt offering. 17 The sacrifices of God are a broken spirit; A broken and a contrite heart, O God, You will not despise.

18 By Your favor do good to Zion; [n]Build the walls of Jerusalem. 19 Then You will delight in]righteous sacrifices, In burnt offering and whole burnt offering; Then young bulls will be offered on Your altar.

Letters convey a sense of intimacy that is less apparent in other forms of communication. This is why it is not uncommon for couples to save their love letters to one another for decades—often found lovingly tied with ribbons in a special box after they die.

Apology letters can convey that same sense of intimacy. Have you ever written or received a letter of apology? I can answer yes to both. I remember a time when a close friend and I hurt each other badly through each of our responses to a difficult and deeply personal situation. Our relationship seemed to be damaged beyond repair. I tried to go to her and make amends (see Matthew 5:23-24) but she refused to talk to me. Romans 12:8 was heavy on my heart:

Do all that you can to live in peace with everyone. (NLT)

Had I done "all that I could" to be at peace with her? My spirit was troubled and I felt I had to do more. So I decided to write my apology and seek her forgiveness in a letter. I poured my heart out. I sealed the letter and mailed it off. And then I waited.

And waited.

And waited.

How hard it was to wait! At last she replied. She accepted my apology and forgave me. She also shared her heart. I felt renewed, restored, revived.

Those letters were intimate, personal and freeing.

This Psalm is such a letter. An intimate, personal letter of apology from David to the God with whom he has an intimate and personal relationship.

Today, spend a little extra time with your journal. Instead of writing a few reflections, compose your own intimate letter to God. Use the words "I," "me," and "my" with abandon. Pour your heart out. Make it personal.

He will reply.

And He won't keep you waiting.

To prepare for writing your letter, listen to "Dear Mr. God" **https://www.youtube.com/watch?v=r3l3GPmCrbI**

Day 37 – Introduction to Theme 6

"Purpose"

Read Verses 13, 14, 15

13 Then I will teach transgressors Your ways, And sinners will be converted to You.

14 Deliver me from bloodguiltiness, O God, the God of my salvation; Then my tongue will joyfully sing of Your righteousness.

15 O Lord, open my lips, That my mouth may declare Your praise.

These are my favorite verses of this Psalm. I love the sense of build-up, anticipation and purpose conveyed.

You know that feeling of anticipation you get when you are reading a great book, watching a riveting movie, or listening to a skilled storyteller? As you become immersed in the story your pulse quickens, you lean a little further forward on your chair. You hold your breath—as your mind forms the question *"Then what? What happens next?"*

In these verses, David speaks about what comes next— after acknowledging both God's holiness and his own sinfulness—after cleansing, inner truth and joy have been experienced, then what?

Yesterday, we reflected on how deeply personal this Psalm is—a love letter to God. And yet, it is more than merely personal. God wants us to experience His cleansing, to know His truth and to live with abundant joy *for a reason*. He has a purpose for us that is bigger than our own welfare. We are intended to have a role in His kingdom. He has a job waiting for us, and all of the pre-work has been designed to get us ready for the "and then."

Our purpose.

That simple phrase, "and then" is filled with hope and possibility. To live *with* purpose you first need courage to *believe* you have a purpose. You need hope.

The biggest casualty for children who experience trauma early in their lives is the loss of hope. This was demonstrated painfully and vividly to me one day while working with a group of third-grade students on an art project. The assignment was to draw a picture depicting what life would be like when they were grown-ups. Prior to the art project we discussed the question, "What do you want to be when you grow up?" Some of the answers included, "a fireman," "a space-ship driver," "a rap star" "a mommy" and "Spider-man."

One little girl sat staring at her paper, and did not pick up a single crayon. I went over and knelt beside her, offering to help her get started. Her words pierced my heart, "I can't do this. I don't have to think about what I will be when I grow up because I won't live to grow up."

This child did not have a terminal illness. But she had a nearly-terminal case of hopelessness brought on by the incessant drumbeat of traumatic incidents that had been the theme song of her young life. She was living with grandparents because one parent had been murdered, another was in prison. A brother had permanent disabilities as a result of being injured in a drive-by shooting. The neighborhood where she lived was riddled with bullet holes and makeshift memorials consisting of teddy bears, candles and balloons marking the spots where children had died. She had no hope or belief that she would ever grow up.

Years later, I was leading a focus group of older teens in foster care. I asked them, "What is one thing you wish social workers and foster parents understood about your experience in foster care?"

One teen said, "They need to help us learn how to dream. Do you realize that no one ever asks a foster kid what they want to be when they grow up? I think they don't even believe that we will grow up."

One person can make the difference. One person can breathe the hope of anticipation, *"and then—what comes next?"* into the life of a child who is dangerously close to giving up.

The loss of hope is devastating. The gift of hope is priceless. When our psalmist turns to the phrase "and then. . . ." he is demonstrating that he has hope and a sense of purpose. He trusts that God has hope in him, in his ability to accomplish that purpose.

What a gift.

Will you pray with me today, *"Lord, give me a clearer sense of purpose. I want people who encounter me to encounter You through me. I want to be a vessel for your Holy Spirit to deliver salvation, cleansing, truth and joy to those who have lost hope. Give me guidance and direction, courage and wisdom for the 'and then'. Amen."*

Do you have a sense of purpose? Do you have a personal mission statement? As you reflect on these questions, writing your responses in your journal, listen to children singing, "Make me an Instrument"
https://www.youtube.com/watch?v=T2QkDUBWA6k

Day 38 – Teach

Read Verse 13

13 Then I will teach transgressors Your ways, And sinners will be converted to You.

Read also Psalm 25:4:

Make me know Your ways, O Lord; Teach me Your paths.

I love to teach.

Long before getting a college degree in Elementary Education, I was of the belief that wherever two or more were gathered it was my responsibility to conduct school. My siblings, cousins and the neighborhood children I babysat all bear witness to this fact.

Since leaving college, my career has been centered on teaching both children and adults. I am utterly confident in my ability to teach on many topics: brain development, childhood trauma, foster care, adoption—even how to make killer lasagna.

But *"Your ways,"* Lord? *"I will teach transgressors Your ways. . . ."* I think that is a little above my pay grade. I'm the one always coming to you, Lord, crying out *"Wash me!" "Scrub me!" "Don't cast me away!" "Make me to know joy!"*

I try to follow Your ways, but I stumble and fall so often, how could I presume to teach them to others? Wouldn't that be a little arrogant?

It would indeed, if teaching God's ways meant that I had arrived at perfect holiness. If it meant that I had all the answers.

Thanks be to God, that is **not** what it means!

When David transitions here with the "And then I will teach" he does not mean, now that I have achieved holiness, been once-and-for-all cleansed of sin and absorbed all of God's truth and wisdom, *then* I will be ready to teach.

No!

What I believe David means is this: "Now that I have been broken open and experienced Your gracious loving kindness, holiness and cleansing; Now that I have experienced the "aha" moments of faith and tuned into to Your truth, wisdom and joy; Now that I understand that this will be a lifelong process of confession and restoration and that I will always be standing in the need of more of Your truth and wisdom—NOW in this posture as a humble, contrite and continual seeker, Now I am ready to teach others Your ways and show them Your path."

In this context, I am reminded of lessons I've learned about teaching over the years. The greatest teachers I ever experienced, those I seek to emulate in my own career, did not view students as vessels to be filled, but rather as fellow travelers on life's journey. They embodied three key qualities:

Great Teachers are Lifelong Learners

Teachers love to learn. They wake up each morning eager to see what new lessons the day has to offer. They learn from books, nature, conversations, technology—in classrooms, dining rooms, waiting rooms, prayer closets and even in mud puddles. Their "learning antenna" is always alert for new material, and they are especially open to ways they can learn from their students. As you've followed this study you've read many quotes and nuggets of wisdom I've gained from my children, grandchildren and others in foster care and juvenile justice who I've been privileged to journey with over the years. Great teachers love to learn and consider it a privilege to share that passion with others.

Great Teachers Facilitate Learning

The best teachers are not lecturers, nor do they see themselves as the holders and keepers of knowledge. Rather, they view their role as a facilitator of learning. The NLT version of Psalm 25:4 says it this way: *"Show me the right path, O Lord; point out the road for me to follow."* Good teachers *show* more than they tell. They point out the path and equip their students to follow it. They understand that students will have many learning styles and they seek the best way to ignite the passion for learning in each student.

Great Teachers Care About Their Students

The teacher's greatest joy comes when the students have their own "aha" moments. They see each student as an individual and care about the whole person—they are invested in their heart and soul as well as their mind. The greatest opportunities for learning occur when the teacher and student have a relationship built on their shared passion for learning and joyful anticipation for the exciting new lessons lying just around the corner as they traverse life's path together.

Will you pray with me today, *"Lord, thank you for being the best example of a Great Teacher. Help me to be open to and excited about the opportunities you provide to teach others Your ways and show them Your paths. May I never lose my love for learning or the joy of sharing what I have learned with others as we sojourn together. Amen."*

Think about your favorite teacher. Make a list in your journal of the qualities and characteristics that you admire about this teacher. Select one or two items on this list and commit yourself to working a little harder this week at developing these characteristics in yourself. As you reflect and write today, enjoy Psalm 25 set to music: "Unto Thee O Lord" (Maranatha Singers):

https://www.youtube.com/watch?v=RYc1sLnsHLY

Day 39 – Convert

Read Verse 13

¹³ *Then I will teach transgressors Your ways, And sinners will be converted to You.*

Read also Acts 26:17(b) -18:

I am sending you, to open their eyes so that they may turn from darkness to light and from the dominion of Satan to God, that they may receive forgiveness of sins and an inheritance among those who have been sanctified by faith in Me.

And Ephesians 4:11-12:

And He gave some as apostles, and some as prophets, and some as evangelists, and some as pastors and teachers, for the equipping of the saints for the work of service, to the building up of the body of Christ;

I'm a teacher, not a preacher.

In yesterday's reflection I talked about my lifelong love of teaching. I love learning and sharing what I learn through teaching. I recognized this character trait in myself long before I recognized that it was a gift from God, of the Holy Spirit, a treasured and humbling gift that I seek to use every day in His service.

But I'm not a preacher. And I'm not an evangelist. And I'm OK with that.

That wasn't always the case.

Within the Christian community, one's value as a Christian is often measured by a number—how many souls did you convert today? Last week? Ever? Can you count them? Can you name them? Can you describe the circumstances in which you led them to faith? Whether you can re-count story upon story of individuals you personally led to Christ or major events where you presided over a mass conversion of hundreds or thousands, you must have these stories to tell. Or your faith is suspect.

In spite of Ephesians 4:11 and other scriptures where it is clear that God gives different gifts to different people, we have elevated evangelism out of this status into an expected, required and essential character trait for all Christians—it is no longer a gift given to *some* but a duty and expectation required of *all*.

And I don't have it.

It was easy for me to feel guilt or shame about this until I really read and understood today's verse - *sinners will be converted to You.* In other translations we see that sinners will *turn to you*, or *return to you*.

This builds hope, courage and confidence. If I have accepted God's unfailing love *and* His thorough cleansing, I have a new clean heart, truth in my innermost being and a life characterized by joy. *And then... sinners will be converted*!

Not by me, but by the unfailing, enduring, unquenchable love of God. As highlighted on Day Thirteen, when I live the renewed life described in this Psalm my very life becomes a prayer and a witness.

Restored, cleansed, unbroken, my life has beauty and purpose within the Kingdom. I am part of the team God will use to bring healing, hope, restoration, forgiveness and yes, even conversion, to others. I will do this not by aspiring to be someone I am not, but rather by following wholly and fully the path God has set before me. Using my gifts with humility and gratitude.

This revelation reminded me of a quote, often attributed to Albert Einstein: *"Everybody is a genius. But if you judge a fish by its ability to climb a tree, it will live its whole life believing that it is stupid."*[7]

Will you pray with me today? *"Lord, thank you for the gifts you have given me and grant me the grace, humility and courage to use my gifts every day to bring Your light to Your people. Amen."*

How has this journey through Psalm 51 inspired, empowered and encouraged you to be a light-bearer by using your own gifts? As you reflect on and write your responses to this question in your journal, listen to this powerful song, "City on the Hill" by Casting Crowns:

https://www.youtube.com/watch?v=xORebSq76to

---

[7] *Quote Investigator.* Web. 9 Feb. 2015.
<http://quoteinvestigator.com/2013/04/06/fish-climb/>.

Day 40 – Sing

Read Verse 14

14 Deliver me from bloodguiltiness, O God, the God of my salvation; Then my tongue will joyfully sing of Your righteousness.

Do an online search for phrases such as "music and emotion," "music and the brain," or "music and the spirit," and you will discover hundreds of links to scholarly articles, scientific research, philosophic musings and personal experiences. Music is, indeed, he universal language that transcends time and space.

Incredible work is being done today in nursing homes, veterans hospitals, domestic violence shelters, mental health facilities, schools for children with autism, child trauma centers and prisons using music as a conduit for restoring the minds, memories and spirits of people who have been deeply wounded, isolated, disconnected from the world around them or even violent.

Most people have their own personal anecdotes attesting to the deeply human experience that music has the power to heal, soothe, inspire, motivate, energize, connect, support learning and more. Nearly all of these benefits are frequently realized even when the melodies play silently in one's own mind, or privately through ear phones—unheard by and unshared with anyone else.

Yet, there is something deeply profound about the *sharing* of music. Expressing it not only in the privacy of your own mind, shower or car, but also in the company of others.

Once a month we take a rag-tag children's choir, consisting of youngsters between the ages of three and twelve, to sing at a local nursing home. The children don't always stay on key, but they do shout out joyfully, singing exultantly to the Lord and their human audience. Residents who rarely communicate and smile even less frequently light up, sing, move and clap along with the children.

Some of the best gifts I have received as a mom and nanna, over the years have been songs given to or dedicated to me by children who had difficulty expressing their emotions any other way. When one particular daughter sent me a cassette tape, years ago, of the song "You are the Wind Beneath My Wings," it marked an important turning point in our relationship, and I played it so often, I wore the tape out.

Our son Dylan, who I have written about in these pages several times before, had limited ability to communicate with others in traditional ways. Music provided the vehicle for relationship building, bonding, laughter and joy to be shared with this precious child. When he passed away, all of our family members gathered to remember Dylan and we compiled a playlist of his favorite music. The tunes on this list range from songs by the Smurfs, to "Amazing Grace." Jazz, R & B, country, classical, gospel and silly parodies ebb and flow together forming the powerful river of his life's story and testimony.

Our passage today reminds us that once our spirits experience the renewed joy only God's healing and restorative power can impart, our natural response is to sing. To sing *aloud.* To sing to be heard, not only in our own heads. The Hebrew word translated as "sing" in this passage is *te rannen,* meaning not only to sing, but to sing aloud, to shout, belt out, lift up one's voice in a resounding song.

What songs comprise the playlist of your own life's story and testimony? Make a list in your journal. For your prayer time today, sing, sing out loud, belt one out for the Lord. Here's a great rendition of "I'm going to Sing when the Spirit Says Sing" to get you started.

https://www.youtube.com/watch?v=OBrVIAZ5qiY

Day 41 – "Open My Lips!"

Read Verse 15

15 O Lord, open my lips, That my mouth may declare Your praise.

Our children don't honor us *every time* they open their mouths. As both a parent and a professional in the trauma field, I know that the old-time punishment, *"I'll wash your mouth out with soap,"* is not only passé and ineffective, it can also be harmful to children. Nevertheless, I confess, there are times when I have been tempted to use it upon hearing the horrid, disrespectful or distasteful things that can come out of the mouths of babes.

In the same way, we don't always honor God with our mouths. James Chapter Three reminds us that *no one can tame the tongue (v. 8)*. I encourage you to read the entire chapter as context for today's reflection.

To help our children learn this lesson, we employed a powerful object lesson one night at the dinner table. We gave each child a square of cardboard and a tube of toothpaste. We placed a ten-dollar bill on the table and announced a contest. *"There will be two parts to the contest, and the winner will receive the ten dollars,"* we told them.

Eagerly, the children waited for direction.

"Part One: When we say 'Go!' squeeze all of the toothpaste out of the tube onto your cardboard as fast as you are able," we instructed. The children rushed to comply, each clearly hoping to finish before their siblings.

After the task was completed, we gave the second instruction, *"Now comes Part Two: Whoever can put all their toothpaste back into the tube will win the ten dollars."*

Crestfallen faces started back at us. A few actually tried before succumbing to defeat. No one was able to claim the prize.

Words are like the toothpaste, once they have escaped our lips, they cannot be *"put back in."* We need to be careful with our words and strive to tame our tongues.

On other occasions, the words of our children honor us greatly. I find I am the proudest of my children when they use their words to speak up for others, particularly for those without voices. God tells us that He, too, is honored when we open our mouths in this way. Consider Proverbs 31: 8-9 *"Open your mouth for the mute. For the rights of all the unfortunate. Open your mouth, judge righteously, defend the rights of the afflicted and needy."*

God seared this passage onto my heart and soul when he led me to Mary, a scared, pregnant 19-year-old girl[8].

I was 22 when I met Mary. I was a recent bride and newly licensed foster parent. A nurse friend asked me to reach out to Mary, who had been hospitalized after a suicide attempt. She had no family.

I visited Mary, gently getting to know her. She began to share her life story, growing up in foster care, but quickly became confused. She couldn't remember all of the places she'd lived or people she'd been told to call "mom" or "dad." Foster homes blurred together until the cold December morning when she woke up in a group home, expecting a day like any other.

When a staff person knocked on her bedroom door telling her to gather her things because she was moving, she didn't flinch. It was a common occurrence in her life. As they walked toward the front door, she asked, "Where am I going this time?"

---

[8] This portion of today's reflection recounting Mary's story was previously published in my book, *No Matter What: A Glimpse into the Heart of Adoption.* Helping Hands, 2014. Print.

He opened the door, looked out upon the snowy winter day and said, "Happy Birthday, Mary! You're 18, you're free of the system now – go anywhere you want."

A year later, she was 19, pregnant and alone.

We cried, hugged and prayed together. I connected her with resources. I'm not sure if her life changed.

But mine was never the same.

With a broken heart, I sank to my knees, sobbing, asking God what I could do to make a difference for all the other Marys – frightened, disconnected and alone.

"Open your mouth for the mute" God said to me, *"For the rights of all the unfortunate. Open your mouth, judge righteously, defend the rights of the afflicted and needy. (Proverbs 31: 8-9)*

We honor God when we open our lips to bring his righteousness and justice into our broken world. This is one of the great purposes we are privileged to carry out each day of our earthly journey.

Will you pray with me today, *"Dear Lord, You gave me the opportunity to open my heart to a scared and lonely girl and she broke it. From that brokenness, You taught me to open my mouth and speak up for lonely, brokenhearted children. Help each of us today to listen to You as you direct us to 'Open Our Lips' on behalf of your children in our midst. Amen."*

When and how has God prompted you to "open your lips" and speak up on behalf of another? How can you be more tuned-in to these opportunities in the future? Make a few notes in your journal as you reflect on these questions, while listening to "I Will Speak Out"

https://www.youtube.com/watch?v=bcyGqgZWZnE

Day 42 – Declare

Read Verse 15

15 O Lord, open my lips, That my mouth may declare Your praise.

Our journey is drawing to a close. We've spent six weeks together, sojourning with David into the depths of our own hearts, and the very heart of God. I've shared stories that hopefully made you laugh, cry, ponder, wonder, think, re-think and deepen your faith.

We began by contemplating God's holiness and unfailing love. This girded us for our weeklong descent into the valley of sin, which separates us from God. Thankfully, God was already preparing hyssop and fluffy towels for us so that we could experience the freshness and power of being completely and thoroughly clean. With our clean hearts and renewed spirits we gained the courage and confidence to know truth in our innermost being and to experience joy like never before. Finally, this week we focused on the potent phrase, *"and then,"* deepening our awareness that our lives have meaning and purpose.

As we prepare to turn the last page and close this book, let us consider how we will live our lives more fully, with greater courage and renewed hope. Are we ready to step out in faith, with steadfast and willing spirits to boldly declare God's praise with every fiber of our being?

Perhaps you, like me, grew up with a grandmother or auntie who liked to use the phrase, *"I do declare!"* This phrase connotes truth, confidence, boldness and perhaps a hint of surprise. In our passage today, God calls us to live our lives in such a way as to *declare* His praise.

A couple of my favorite definitions of the word *declare* include: *"to say in a strong and confident way,"* and *"to make evident."*[9] The original Hebrew word, *nagad*, as defined in Strong's Concordance[10] means, *"to be conspicuous."*

We declare God's praise not by speaking in pious or holier-than-thou language. Not by taking after the Scribes and Pharisees that Jesus took to task in Matthew chapter twenty-three for their pretentious utterings and other forms of hypocrisy. Not by lacing every conversation with Bible passages, chapter and verse.

No.

We declare God's praise when we confidently live in a way that makes the fruits of the spirit conspicuous and evident. *"But the fruit of the Spirit is love, joy, peace, patience, kindness, goodness, faithfulness, gentleness, self-control; against such things there is no law." Galatians 5:22-23*

When we have the confidence that comes from the clean heart, steadfast spirit, and renewed joy discovered along the path of our Psalm 51 journey we are able to declare God's praise by showing love, kindness, peace and all of the other fruits of the spirit to anyone we encounter—whether a traumatized child, an unreasonable boss, a stressed-out spouse, a homeless or mentally ill individual, a person who looks, thinks, speaks or acts differently than we do; in short anyone and everyone.

Be bold.

Be conspicuous.

Live it. Declare it.

Please join me in praying, *"Lord, give me the confident courage to declare Your praises in the way I live my life, by showing your love, kindness and peace to all. By remaining steadfast in my spirit and spreading the joy you have placed in my heart. By trusting your truth and the unending, unfailing nature of your love. Give me the wisdom to know*

---

[9] *Merriam-Webster.* Merriam-Webster. Web. 9 Feb. 2015. <http://www.merriam-webster.com/dictionary/declare>.

[10] *Strong's Hebrew: 5046. נָגַד (nagad) -- to Be Conspicuous.* Web. 9 Feb. 2015. <http://biblehub.com/hebrew/5046.htm>.

when to turn back to you for another scrubbing with heavenly hyssop, the courage to open my mouth on behalf of your precious children and the grace to walk humbly with you from day to day. Thank you for the wisdom in Psalm 51 and throughout your scriptures. Thank you for creating a clean heart in me today and every day. Amen.

Let's end our journey with two songs. First, "Love Each Other" by Graham Kendrick as we contemplate on today's reflection.

https://www.youtube.com/watch?v=2MblrWZDpPQ

And finally, come around full circle and listen once again to Keith Green, "Create in Me A Clean Heart" as we did on the first day of our time together.

https://www.youtube.com/watch?v=rv16YUTCp9U&feature=kp

As you listen to these two songs, return to the questions and prayers we started with on Day One: Ask God to give you eyes to see and ears to hear Psalm 51 anew as if reading it for the first time. Take a few minutes to write in your journal – what are your "first-impressions-all-over-again" of this Psalm? What is one hope you have for how God will speak to you and renew your spirit during this season of reflection?

Add some notes today reflecting on your heart-response to these questions. How did God speak to you in these six weeks? In what ways was your spirit renewed? What lessons do you walk away with? What "aha" moments will you remember?